Controversies

Controversies

A dialogue on the politics and philosophy of
our times

Alain Badiou
Jean-Claude Milner

Moderated by Philippe Petit

Translated by Susan Spitzer

polity

First published in French as *Controverse* © Éditions du Seuil, 2012

This English edition © Polity Press, 2014

Polity Press
65 Bridge Street
Cambridge CB2 1UR, UK

Polity Press
350 Main Street
Malden, MA 02148, USA

ISBN-13: 978-0-7456-8216-7
ISBN-13: 978-0-7456-8217-4(pb)

A catalogue record for this book is available from the British Library.

Typeset in 11 on 13 pt Sabon
by Toppan Best-set Premedia Limited
Printed and bound in Great Britain by T.J. International Ltd,
Padstow, Cornwall

The publisher has used its best endeavors to ensure that the URLs for external websites referred to in this book are correct and active at the time of going to press. However, the publisher has no responsibility for the websites and can make no guarantee that a site will remain live or that the content is or will remain appropriate.

Every effort has been made to trace all copyright holders, but if any have been inadvertently overlooked the publisher will be pleased to include any necessary credits in any subsequent reprint or edition.

For further information on Polity, visit our website: www.politybooks.com

Contents

Unreconciled

Philippe Petit

Here are two giants, two French intellects who are frequently denounced, and never for the same reasons. They met in 1967, during the "Red Years" in Paris. Badiou was a *lycée* teacher at the time; Milner had just returned from a year at MIT. The former is now the most widely read contemporary French thinker abroad; the latter, who is largely unknown there, has become a leading intellectual figure in France.

Both share an unconditional love for the French language and its own particular dialectic. They hadn't compared their careers and ideas since they broke off relations in 2000 as a result of an article by Alain Badiou in the French daily *Libération* that had rubbed Jean-Claude Milner the wrong way. In that article, Badiou had lampooned the trajectory of Benny Lévy (1945–2003), a former comrade-in-arms and friend of Milner who had gone, as is well known, or as he himself put it, "from Moses to Mao and from Mao to Moses." They had never really discussed their differences in such a head-on way.

So there was nothing inevitable about the exchange the reader will find in these pages between Alain Badiou, born in 1937 in Rabat, Morocco, and Jean-Claude Milner, born in 1941 in Paris. It might well have broken off as they went along. It was therefore agreed by both parties that it would be carried out to its conclusion, that they wouldn't let it get bogged down in posturing, and that it would deal as much with the issues of our times as with each one's system of thought. It would moreover be an opportunity for them to set out their quarrels over time and justify their assumptions. And, finally, it would provide a summary, when read, of the differences between the speaker and the spoken to, without ever losing sight of those they were addressing.

To that end, a protocol had to be established. It was decided that we would meet four times, between January and June 2012. During the first three sessions we sat on a sofa and armchairs and, during the last one, around a table, something I had requested in order to vary the mode of interlocution and to be able to spread out my papers – but in reality so as to moderate the dialogue as much as possible. Jean-Claude Milner wryly remarked that he was afraid of being "devoured" by this system, the way Kierkegaard was by Hegel. Was it because of the table? The nature of the topics covered? Whatever the case, the last session was by far the most relaxed one. During the conversation – and it really was one – they treated each other with kid gloves.

These meetings had been arranged over a lunch during which a short summary of the points of friction between the two thinkers was addressed. The infinite was one of them, as were the universal and the name "Jew."[1] But the discussion turned fairly quickly into a high-quality international press review.

[1] The English translation of the French noun *nom*, as used here in "*le nom 'juif'*," is problematic. *Nom* can refer, variously, to a name, a noun, or a word. An interviewer once asked Milner what he meant by "*nom*," adding: "Perhaps you might also take into account the

The scene could have been set in an embassy library, but it actually took place in a restaurant near Notre-Dame. Alain Badiou and Jean-Claude Milner had just gotten back in touch with each other. That day, they exchanged their views on Germany and Europe, American campuses, and French political life, though they didn't bring up the Middle East. It didn't matter, however, since the dialogue between them, focusing on theoretical issues and based on concrete analyses, had been renewed. All that needed to be done was to guide and moderate it to keep it from going awry.

The sessions lasted three hours each and took place as agreed. Rereading the discussions proved to be a particularly fruitful task. Each of the authors reviewed and revised his contribution, leaving the rhythm of the discussions unchanged but making the wording clearer in some places.

In the transition from the spoken to the written word each one's arguments were tightened and their positions made more forceful. The conversational tone, in which long developments alternated with snappier, more staccato-like responses, was nevertheless preserved in the final product, which reflects the quality of the listening, the sense of surprise, and the desire to convince that had emerged in the face-to-face meetings.

question of the names for '*nom*' in English, that is to say, what we call the name and the noun." Milner replied: "And how to translate it" (Ann Banfield and Daniel Heller-Roazen, "Interview with Jean-Claude Milner," *Journal of the Jan Van Eyck Circle for Lacanian Ideology Critique* 3 (2010), 14–15). Badiou, in contrast, tends to use *mot* ("word") for the same purposes (see, in particular, his "Portées du mot 'juif'" in *Circonstances 3*, translated by Steven Corcoran as "Uses of the Word 'Jew'," in *Polemics* [London and New York: Verso, 2006.]). Indeed, in the Postscript to this book, where political names in general are discussed at some length, Badiou challenges Milner about his choice of terminology before agreeing to use *nom* for the sake of argument. Given this concession, I have translated *nom* as "name" throughout.
Translator's note: All footnotes in this translation are my own.

For if there is no thinking without a division at once internal and external to the subject, just as there is no violence that is not both subjective and objective, there can be no true dialogue unless the assumptions and method of each of the participants are broached. Just being opposed to each other is not enough; the other person still has to be convinced, and, when that can't happen, simply defending oneself is not enough; one must be able to justify the grounds for one's arguments. This, I believe, is something that Alain Badiou and Jean-Claude Milner pulled off perfectly in this dialogue. They argued, very heatedly at times – to the point of requesting that a postscript be added regarding what bothered them the most, namely, their respective positions on the State of Israel and the situation of the Palestinians – and they went head to head on key issues, such as the status of the universal, the name "Jew," mathematics, and the infinite. But they also pooled their opinions, or, rather, harmonized their thinking, on a number of points having to do with the legacy of revolutions, Marx's work, international law, the Arab uprisings, the historical situation of France, the role of the parliamentary left, the so-called "normal" presidential candidate,[2] the *Indignés* movement, Nicolas Sarkozy's legacy, and many other issues as well.

They agreed, as it were, on their disagreement and didn't hesitate to agree on everything else. They had to do so, in order to avoid taking the easy way out and creating the impression that there was some subtext of friendly understanding between them to set off each of their careers to advantage. For it is a given of French intellectual history that it is unlike any other. It is not better than the others, nor does it reflect an indifference

---

[2]In the 2012 French presidential campaign, François Hollande, the Socialist candidate, in reaction to Nicolas Sarkozy's so-called "bling-bling presidency," pledged to be "a normal candidate for a normal presidency."

to anything foreign, but it is driven by its own principle of division. Thus, Descartes – that French knight[3] – is no more French than Pascal, and Rousseau, in terms of his language, is no less so than Voltaire, *pace* Péguy and all those who despaired of finding an appropriate phrase to define *l'esprit français*, whose lightness Nietzsche wanted so desperately to capture.

There is nothing to hope for from such ridiculous essentialism. Nevertheless, we should properly appreciate what sets French intellectual history apart in terms of its style and thought. Sartre was at once an implacable ideologist and a peerless analyst of political tensions, a writer in the tradition of the French moralists and a committed intellectual in the strongest sense of the term. Alain Badiou is a philosopher through and through, a staunch advocate of clear writing, and a gifted lecturer; he is both a writer and someone true to his commitments. His father, a member of the Resistance who would analyze for his son the Allied armies' advances on a map on his office wall and would become mayor of Toulouse after the Liberation, was his first mentor. Sartre and Althusser were his first masters, and those public agitators, the Enlightenment *philosophes*, were a constant source of inspiration to him. There's not a line of his work that isn't indebted to these diverse traditions, to which must be added the names of Plato and Lacan, who tie together his idea of truth and his conception of the subject.

Nothing can be understood about the development of his work, his metaphysics, and his recent entry into the public debate if he is not interpreted against that

---

[3]In his *Note conjointe sur Monsieur Descartes et la philosophie cartésienne* (1914), Charles Péguy wrote: "In the history of thought, Descartes will always be the French knight who took off at such a good pace." Cited in Jacques Derrida, *Adieu to Emmanuel Lévinas*, trans. Pascale-Anne Brault and Michael Naas (Stanford, CA: Stanford University Press, 1999), 139, n. 43.

background. The reason that Alain Badiou is a global thinker today, an international philosopher as well known in Argentina as he is in Belgium, Greece, or California, has as much to do with that legacy as with his ability to keep it at arm's length. There is, in fact, a big difference between the way he is viewed on the banks of the Seine and the way he is viewed on the banks of the Thames. Speaking in English wherever the need arises, translating into English what Beckett strove to express in French, he realizes how little the role he plays here or is made to play elsewhere corresponds to his particular situation.

Although different, the mark the war left on Jean-Claude Milner's background was also a decisive one. His father, a Jew of Lithuanian descent, was a habitué of Montparnasse. He was a bon vivant, sparing with his memories and reticent about his activities. Denounced by a neighbor during the Occupation years, he managed to avoid the worst by joining the STO [Compulsory Work Service]. But it was only around the age of 15, and by putting two and two together, that Milner figured out that his father was Jewish, since he had considered the word to be meaningless, except in the minds of anti-Semites. His aunt died in the Warsaw ghetto. A close friend of his parents who returned to France in 1946 had been deported to Auschwitz.

This background weighed heavily on his formative years and had a profound impact on his intellectual career, although not to the point of preventing the teenager he was from living his life, being enamored of frivolous novels and indulging in reading Rosamond Lehmann, or of being totally overwhelmed by his father's reticence.

We shouldn't be too quick to rely on personal anecdotes, however. And it would be wrong to reduce this dispute to a mere difference of temperaments or personal histories, unless we accept that the biographeme, or protohistory, coincides with the whole curve of life, like body temperature or the silence of the organs;[4] or that contingency is all and the original choice is nothing; or that social determinations are the be-all and end-all and "the unfathomable decision of being" (Lacan) just some psychoanalyst's whim. In the cases of Jean-Claude Milner and Alain Badiou there are certainly explanatory frameworks rooted in early childhood or youth. But let's not exaggerate. Sartre's and Camus's tumultuous relationship can no more be reduced to a quarrel between a curly-haired Parisian petty bourgeois and a poor boy playing soccer with the kids of Mondovi in Algeria than the tempestuous friendship between these two epigones of May '68 can be reduced to a titanic struggle between Badiou's glorious father and Milner's erratic one – let alone their mothers, who would only serve to corroborate the analysis.

To assume that a person's life can either enhance or tarnish their work is the mark of a litigious mind, certainly not of inspired thinking. Such an attitude cynically imposes the perspective of death on life. It obfuscates what may yet come from these two great men whose work is not yet complete and whom it would be wrong to set in stone. Jean-Claude Milner, who admits in *L'Arrogance du présent* (2009) that he fulfilled the "duty of infidelity," ought to know. The choice he made to devote himself to structural linguistics rather than to philosophy, even though he felt genuine admiration – as did Alain Badiou – for Lacan and Althusser, still weighs on him today. It represented an initial career orientation that was a unique way for him to enter the world of the French language, endure its silences, acquire the vocabulary of the French Revolution, and avoid becoming "the present's servant," meaning someone who, in his view, is merely the mouthpiece of the "unlimited society," or, if you prefer, the symptom of smug progressivism, which

---

[4]A French surgeon, René Leriche (1879–1955), defined health as "life lived in the silence of the organs."

only cares about the weak if they stay in their place and don't unduly disturb its appetite for power, conquest, and concealed domination.

That original choice, at any rate, defined the horizon of this dialogue with regard to the fate of the French language, "a dead language" today for Jean-Claude Milner, just as the history of France is "on its last legs" for Alain Badiou. Because if there was one topic – and this is no accident – on which our two dialogue partners agreed, could relate to each other, and came together, it was the topic with the name "France," whose history is allegedly disappearing – to parody Michel Foucault – "like a face drawn in sand at the edge of the sea."[5] To such an extent, in fact, that it is giving way, on this now faceless beach, to a divisive name – "French," as it happens – "which individuals and groups have a duty to resemble as closely as possible if they are to merit positive attention from the State."[6] Or, to put it another way, it is providing the key to the secret behind the calm[7] that was promised on this beach stripped of the name "France," namely, the revenge of the "spirit of '68," which "became the Restoration's staunchest ally."[8]

So that was the end point of this dialogue taking stock of our recent history. Whether it was a question of the left and the right, neither of which Jean-Claude Milner thinks is defined by "values"; or of Nicolas Sarkozy's legacy; or of the specific character of the

---

[5]In *The Order of Things* (New York: Vintage, 1973), Foucault famously predicted that man would disappear "like a face drawn in sand at the edge of the sea" (p. 387). Milner refers to this quotation in his *Les Penchants criminels de l'Europe démocratique* (Paris: Verdier, 2003).

[6]Alain Badiou, *The Rebirth of History*, trans. Gregory Elliott (London and New York: Verso, 2012), 97.

[7]The calm in question is the one that has "prevailed in France over the past 40 years," as Milner explains in *L'Arrogance du présent* (Paris: Grasset & Fasquelle, 2009), 236.

[8]*L'Arrogance du présent*, 237.

French government machine, which can run only on condition of the reconciliation of the power elite (see below, pp. 113 ff.); or of the foretold death of the left-wing intellectual, a host of artificial oppositions were shattered here under the impact of the exchange. Even the opposition between moderns and anti-moderns was rendered obsolete.

After they both left the dead planet of revolution, by different routes, to be sure, they realized that the revolution was henceforth a matter of tradition. The end of the revolution marked its final destination, but certainly not the end of that goal. Thus, after reading this discussion, it is finally possible to be modern without having contempt for tradition, as Michel Crépu wrote of Chateaubriand.[9] Since the duty of transmission is the guarantee of the future, there is no longer even any need to oppose the past to the future to make it exist. The classic is no longer someone who is opposed to revolution or progress and recycles the past into pointless, boring folklore, but instead someone who reshapes the past and restores to it its share of experiences and failures so as to give innovation a chance. What kind of chance, though? Here is where the classics part company. And, not surprisingly, a theme that runs through this whole heated exchange, which began by recalling an earlier, original dispute, returns at the end.

Jean-Claude Milner and Alain Badiou did not, in fact, leave the planet Revolution aboard the same spaceship. And there is no common measure between Milner's abandonment of the political worldview and Badiou's ongoing pursuit of it. This exchange is thus first and foremost an invitation to a reading of the "century of revolutions," as Antoine Vitez called it, of the century of communism. It is a reading for two voices, which allows us to reject or accept – it all depends – the anti-totalitarian approach as much as the sequential

[9] Michel Crépu, *Le Souvenir du monde: Essai sur Chateaubriand* (Paris: Grasset, 2011).

approach, according to which, after the failure of the cycle of revolutions, there would come an "in-between" period when an emancipatory vision of history might be reinstated.

In this respect, the exchange is a follow-up to an earlier debate that took an unexpected turn upon the publication, in 1992, of *Constat*, a book that marked a major turning point in Jean-Claude Milner's career. The discussion at that time was about the unintelligibility of the name "politics" and the status of the infinite as it was bound up with revolutionary fervor and the progress the French Revolution had brought about. Milner's rejection of maximal behaviors, henceforth severed, in his opinion, from both rebellion and thought, led to a disagreement that was never resolved. Ever since then, the skepticism of the author of *La Politique des choses* has constantly run up against the doctrinal passion of the philosopher Alain Badiou.

That incipient debate couldn't be allowed to come to nothing. After the death of Guy Lardreau[10] in 2008, Jean-Claude Milner reconnected with Alain Badiou, who three years later would come up with the idea of this *disputatio*. But how could the debate be resumed? What basis could be provided for the question, inasmuch as it was addressed to this other person who still wanted to "change the world"? "Let's be clear-headed and sensible!" said one of them. "Let's formulate hypotheses!" said the other. With an alternative like that, it was a given that Lucretius' admirer would bang heads with Plato's heir. Weren't Milner's minimalist arguments actually a sort of challenge to the maximalist propositions of the author of *Logics of Worlds*?

---

[10]The philosopher Guy Lardreau (1947–2008) was one of the co-founders, in 1968, of the Maoist Gauche Prolétarienne organization. His book *L'Ange* (Paris: Grasset, 1976), co-authored with Christian Jambet, later became a founding text of the "new philosophy."

Likewise, the latter's "communist hypothesis" beto-
kened a final attack on the renegades of the so-called
"new philosophy," who, in Milner's case at least, had
assumed the mantle not of an abandonment of thinking
but of anti-philosophy, or, to be more precise, of a subtle
pragmatism in which were combined a fierce rejection
of violence on behalf of history's massacres and an
unsparing view of his opposite number's bold aberra-
tions. Until the name "Jew" – and what it implies in
terms of the universal's status – intervened and reopened
the quarrel, this time for good.

The quarrel needed to be reopened and the issues
defined. It had to be put back on a track that could only
be determined through the apparatus of thought of
these two children of war. "Apparatus" must be understood to mean something a little more than equipment
or armor, since when two classics meet and discuss the
future, what's at issue is not same-sex marriage but the
type of access they have to the real. When Jean-Claude
Milner says, "I don't have an affirmative ontology" and
Alain Badiou replies that there may be a local conver-
gence of an affirmative ontology and a "dispersive
ontology," given that in both instances the world is
presented to us in the guise of multiplicity, the importance of that exchange should not be underestimated. It
marked the beginning of the massive disagreement that
developed as the dispute went on. It introduced an
acknowledgment that, although mutual at the beginning, was only as good as its consequences, as the
adventure of thought that spawned the disagreement
and fueled it, until it produced the formulation: "The
twentieth century took place."[11] The crisis of traditional
politics is the proof of this. On that they agreed, it is
ironic to note, but their respective interpretations of

[11] This sentence, credited to the novelist and political activist Natacha
Michel, originally appeared in Badiou's *The Century* (Cambridge,
UK and Malden, MA: Polity, 2007), xiii; translation modified.

what was meant by it differed. For Jean-Claude Milner, the hard kernel of politics is the possible killing, and the survival, of bodies, whereas for Alain Badiou it is "the historical process of the collective correlation between equality and freedom," as well as the possible return to the understanding of mass murders.

Thus, there was a total lack of agreement between them about the "terrible twentieth century"[12] and its aftermath. Jean-Marie Straub and Danièle Huillet's second film, which opened in theaters in 1965, was entitled *Unreconciled (Nicht versöhnt* in German). The title fits these two intellectuals who strode boldly through the last century to a tee. It accurately captures their desire not to sell their experience short, as though that century's violence were still permeating their current thinking and it was the responsibility of both of them to inform the public that they would not accept a degraded present; that it was important to question whether the petty bourgeois intelligentsia still had a future; that there were at least two ways of examining its exit from history – definitive for Milner, temporary for Badiou – and that it was possible to cultivate the difference between two related yet opposed conceptions of transmission.

Two giants, as I called them, worlds apart from each other, but whom I nonetheless brought together. Two unreconciled authentic thinkers who have lost none of their argumentative spirit, which they have no intention of giving up any time soon, and who peer into the world of the future armed with this shared vision: "For to end yet again."[13]

September 2012

---

[12]The phrase was originally Winston Churchill's.
[13]This is the title of a short prose work by Samuel Beckett, implying, perhaps, the impossibility of attaining final closure.

1

An Original Dispute

PHILIPPE PETIT: *Alain Badiou and Jean-Claude Milner, I'm very pleased to be moderating this conversation between the two of you. I'm aware of your mutual distrust of "media hype" and of your tendency to want to escape from a certain consensus. But that doesn't negate the fact that there are profound differences between your intellectual itineraries and worldviews. What I have in mind is primarily your approaches to politics in general and to Plato in particular and your views of history, universality, and the "name 'Jew.'" I also have in mind your relationship or lack thereof to mathematics, as well as the question of the subject and the infinite. But I believe there's no disagreement between you when it comes to the end of the cycle of revolutions, the role of the left today, or France's place in the world. So I'd like for this dialogue to be an opportunity for you to flesh out these differences and areas of agreement. I'd also like for it to be not just an opportunity for you to prolong a war of positions, but for each of you to go into greater detail about your thinking. The adjective "radical" has by now become a form of linguistic shorthand to refer to anyone who rejects voting or doesn't reduce thinking to mere commentary on the world as it is. So, before we get into all these subjects, we can begin by recalling the circumstances of your first meeting and your shared and individual itineraries.*

ALAIN BADIOU: Our first meeting dates from a rather distant past. It was in connection with the review *Cahiers pour l'analyse* [1966–9], of which Jean-Claude Milner was one of the founders. I worked for it later, through the mediation of François Regnault.[1] That was when Jean-Claude Milner and I first got to know each other and began discussing things together. It was the time of our encounter, but the time of our disagreements followed almost immediately thereafter. Our respective involvement in and reactions to May '68 and its aftermath, in particular our positions vis-à-vis the Gauche Prolétarienne organization [1968–70], were very different. I won't go into detail about this now, but it's interesting to note that we had scarcely met before our seemingly joint endeavor was overshadowed by an extremely sharp conflict between us.

JEAN-CLAUDE MILNER: It was a serious disagreement.

AB: A very serious disagreement, with very harsh texts and articles on both our parts. Disputation was already the name of the game. It's interesting that it was there almost from the start.

---

[1] François Regnault (b. 1938) is the author, with Jean-Claude Milner, of *Dire le vers* and of *Conférences d'esthétique lacanienne*, among other works. A member of *Cahiers pour l'analyse* and the Cercle d'épistémologie from their inception, he became a close friend of Alain Badiou in the late 1960s. He taught philosophy at the then-new experimental university, Paris-VIII, at Vincennes and later moved to the Department of Psychoanalysis at Saint-Denis. Regnault has long been involved in theater, founding his own company in 1974, translating many plays, and writing seminal texts on theater.

PP: *What did it involve?*

JCM: On an anecdotal level, I see an initial disagreement about whether or not we would continue with *Cahiers pour l'analyse* after May '68. I was in favor of not continuing with it, while Alain Badiou thought it was possible to do so. The example he gave at the time was the piano, as some Chinese Cultural Revolution ideologues had analyzed it: there was a revolutionary use of the piano, they said, so playing the piano could continue to be pursued in the service of the Revolution.

AB: And since *Cahiers pour l'analyse* was an excellent piano, which was played by Jacques Lacan, Jacques Derrida, Serge Leclaire, Louis Althusser, and I could go on . . .

JCM: My position was linked to the conviction, which I've always had, that if you do something, you do it in its purest form, and if that purest form no longer corresponds to the situation, then you stop.

In addition to this initial disagreement between us there were our totally different ways of becoming involved in Maoism. Badiou always had a relationship with Maoism – or such was my impression, at any rate – that was based on a deliberate, studied, informed familiarity with the Chinese texts (Mao's and those of the various participants in the Cultural Revolution), whereas what I was interested in wasn't China, to which I was ultimately pretty indifferent. So there you have two completely different ways of getting involved.

The third point of divergence between us, it seems to me, was the different relationship to Marxism we each had. What interested me about the Gauche Prolétarienne was the idea that Marxism had reached a new stage – the third stage – which was bringing about changes, the end of Marxism-Leninism, in fact, while

Badiou was quite skeptical about that. I can remember articles he wrote in which he was highly critical of the notion of a new stage, a third stage, and so on. The irony was that we both became involved in Maoism as a result of May '68, but not in the same way. In fact, we became involved in it in opposite ways and with opposite choices of organizations. Everything that happened afterward – this became clear only later on – was determined by our diametrically opposed opinions about Benny Lévy, who was the leader of the Gauche Prolétarienne and followed the itinerary everyone knows. Badiou criticized his ultimate destination as being a sign that something was wrong in the first phase of his itinerary.

AB: I did in fact see that there was a consistency, which was nearly explicit moreover, between the way the leaders of the Gauche Prolétarienne had rallied to Maoism and the way they later abandoned not just Maoism but also any vision of organized revolutionary action, the goal of communism, and even, ultimately, politics *tout court*. The form taken by their abandonment of active politics after the dissolution of the Gauche Prolétarienne in 1972 completely justified, in retrospect, the feeling I had that their espousal of Maoism was largely, to put it in mild terms, a transitory fiction, or, to put it in the style of those times, a sham. That's why Jean-Claude is right to say that there's a line of continuity between him and me extending from the original difference in the way we each got involved in Maoism to the even sharper conflicts between us that resulted from what was, for the leaders of the Gauche Prolétarienne, the abandonment of Maoism.

The odd thing is that, in this history, at each of its stages, the extreme radicalism – or at least that's my perception – was on Jean-Claude Milner's part. I've always had an image of myself as a moderate. At the beginning, I thought a synthesis could be achieved between the continuation of the *Cahiers pour l'analyse* and the consequences of May '68, which was not something Jean-Claude Milner thought. Next, I thought that Maoism was a creative variation in the vast history of communist thought and action, while Jean-Claude Milner claimed it was an absolutely new, unprecedented stage. And, at the end, I thought we could carry on with the political project of emancipation and its accompanying philosophy, while Jean-Claude Milner thought all of that was good only for the junk heap.

JCM: Clearly, there's a difference of views between us as to the notion of synthesis. Without in the least attributing to Badiou the use of the infamous triad "thesis–antithesis –synthesis," I think I can nevertheless detect a moment of synthesis in him, a desire for synthesis, which constantly recurs in a variety of forms. As regards the relationship between politics and philosophy, for example, he thinks that "politics can be thought through philosophy," whereas I think politics can be thought, but not through philosophy. The same goes for the relationship between philosophy and mathematics, and I could give other examples. By contrast, my approach is always a divisive one. I can set up homologies between different discourses, but these homologies aren't syntheses.

PP: *No doubt. That explains why you don't share Alain Badiou's feeling that we're seeing a "rebirth of history" these days, even if you're very attentive to the Arab uprisings and the global effects of the 2008 economic crisis. But this disagreement over synthesis is hardly the only one of your differences or convergences regarding Marx, whom it seems necessary to read again, given the role of the state as agent of capitalism.*

JCM: I think one thing's abundantly clear: the core of classical Marxist analysis has become relevant again. In other words, the – let's call it neoliberal, or at any rate strictly economistic – alternative has collapsed before our very eyes. It's clear that the hard kernel of classical Marxist analysis is by far the most useful tool for understanding what's going on. The other issue is whether or not what's happened before our very eyes in the so-called "Arab revolutions" corresponds to the Marxist model of what's termed a "revolution," but that's another problem.

AB: I'm inclined to agree with Jean-Claude Milner about this. It's undeniable that there's a sort of Marxist obviousness about what's structuring the general history of the world, the crisis and everything that goes with it, today. There has been a spectacular return of Marxism's analytical effectiveness. It's true that a certain "Marxism" had long been incorporated within general ideology. Theories that, when I was a schoolboy, were still severely criticized by teachers and in textbooks, such as the primacy of the economy, the fact that it's the determining factor, and so on, became, over time, accepted theories, clichés of ideological debate. It's a little different today. What we're being reminded of is a lot more precise. It's the cyclical nature of crises, the possibility of certain systemic collapses, the relationship between finance capitalism and industrial capitalism, the role of the state as a rescuer in periods of crisis – governments as agents of capitalism – and also the horizon of war that all this may imply. All these phenomena are being thought through by a revised, expanded analytical Marxism. But as for determining what political conclusions can be drawn from these analytical observations, when it's a question of determining whether or not the huge processes of riot and revolt going on here and there in the context of the crisis are opening up perspectives comparable to the ones envisioned by the politics that claimed to be Marxist, well, that's a different kettle of fish. Between systemic analysis and political clarification there's no transitivity.

JCM: The issue is even more different, and here I'm coming to Marx himself, in that he was always at a loss when it came to the revolutionary movements he himself witnessed. At first he was at a loss, but before long he developed a discourse. Take the Paris Commune, for example. After some time had gone by, he grasped at straws until he eventually came up with a discourse that explained what was going on. What he wrote is still interesting, but it's really separate from his overall doctrine. The question you're asking about Marx could be asked instead about Marxism-Leninism, the Leninist reinterpretation of Marx. Lenin supplemented the hard kernel of Marx's analysis with a doctrine that established the criteria for identifying what a "revolution" is, what isn't one, and what the obligatory points of passage, the markers, and so forth, are. The coupling of *Capital* and the theory of revolutions, which we owe to Lenin, is Marxism-Leninism properly speaking. For the time being, nothing going on in the world strikes me as reviving Marxism-Leninism.

AB: If what's meant by "Marxism-Leninism" is the ossified doctrine of what I call the "old Marxism," namely, the application of a fixed bunch of academic categories to all different sorts of situations, then I, too, think that such "Marxism-Leninism" has no chance of reviving, however serious the crisis of capitalism may be. As Jean-Claude Milner has moreover suggested, that kind of "Marxism-Leninism" was already undermined by Maoism, by numerous political innovations that came out of the Cultural Revolution, in particular the fact that thinking a situation is only possible by actively linking up with its players, whether they be young revolutionaries, striking workers, or peasants forced off their lands, and that therefore the categories of politics presuppose new forms of relationship between the intellectuals and what the Chinese called the "broad masses." Nowadays, the "old Marxism," academic Marxism, is even more moribund than it was in the 1960s. However, the possibility that the current revolts may be related in some way to a conception of the movement of history that privileges the masses, their effective mobilization, and their revolutionary unpredictability, is another matter altogether. To refine this kind of hypothesis, you have to investigate on site. As Mao said, "No investigation, no right to speak."

PP: *So you both acknowledge the validity of analytical Marxism, but you completely disagree about what to think about the type of political organization that would be desirable nowadays . . .*

JCM: We may well be touching on a profound difference between us here. Personally, I have long thought that there could be no theoretical agreement between us on the answer to the question: "What should the political organization be in a particular situation?" I'm completely pragmatic in this regard. Something that may be appropriate for a couple of months can stop being so a couple of months later. When I say politics can be thought, it doesn't mean that political organization can be thought.

AB: Oddly enough, if we confine ourselves to what Jean-Claude Milner just said, I don't disagree. There's no universally acceptable or legitimate theory today of what a political organization dedicated to the emancipation of humanity, or to be more precise, guided by the communist Idea, is. As regards the question of communist organization, there were essentially three stages. First, there was Marx's vision, according to which, as he explained in the *Manifesto*, it was a matter of organizing, at an international level, an ideological movement within the global history of uprisings. Communists, for Marx, were a part of the workers' movement. This is a historicist vision of political organization: it's not something separate, it's an educated component of the history of revolution and it clarifies that history's future stages and global dimension. Next, there was the Leninist phase. By giving Marx a very sharp twist, Lenin proposed the building of an essentially militarized organization, which is to say a separate organization, capable of commanding either insurrectional or prolonged civil war-type confrontations. In any case, this kind of organization had to respect principles such as "iron discipline," hierarchy, the ability to go underground, and so on. These principles proved to be very effective when it came to taking power and taking control of the state, after a whole century of worker revolts that were put down with bloodshed. Those victories then met with a tremendous, totally justified response. Where the long-term construction of a new society aspiring to real communism was concerned, however, the "Party form" invented by Lenin showed its limitations. Merging communist politics and the dictatorial state, it combined inertia and terror.

So, as far as the issue of organization goes, it's fair to say that the first two stages, as we know, are over. Marxism-Leninism collapsed during the period of the socialist states' delegitimation. The Cultural Revolution, one of Maoism's amazing initiatives, was an attempt, within the second stage, to save its principles and its future by redirecting it toward communism through the mobilization of the masses, if need be against the sclerotic party, which Mao boldly referred to as the "new bourgeoisie." However, as that revolution failed, we're somewhat at a loss with regard to the problems it dealt with, which are still our problems. As a result, the difference of opinion between Jean-Claude and me isn't about whether there exists a formal theory of communist political organization today, but about whether it matters if there is one or not. The conclusion that I think was Benny Lévy's, and is ultimately Jean-Claude Milner's, is that this issue is no longer important at all. So I interpret that position as a pure and simple adoption of political skepticism.

PP: *Or at any rate as an adoption of his critique of the political worldview.*

AB: Jean-Claude Milner's whole assessment of this experience, an experience which in a certain way the two of us shared, at any rate between 1968 and 1971, amounts to saying that there is no – and in reality that there cannot be any – theory of political organization. It's an overall skeptical assessment of the first two stages involved, as ventures inscribed in the Cultural Revolution, which can be summed up philosophically by saying that politics is not really a thought, that there's nothing in it but its local pragmatics. I, for my part, of course think that the first two stages of communist politics are over, but I still claim that politics is a thought and that we will invent the political organization of the third stage. Once again, we have similar diagnoses of the problem but completely different treatments for it.

PP: *Jean-Claude Milner, you mentioned "pragmatism." Is that a result of your skepticism?*

JCM: Yes, but I'd use the term "skepticism" in a strong sense, that is, a skepticism in the ancient sense of the term, not a benign skepticism. It's a skeptical position vis-à-vis politics as organization. Hence, pragmatism and maybe even acceptance of bricolage – with diagnoses that are always short term, something that doesn't preclude my making predictions. To go back to the question of the Arab revolutions, the Tahrir Square episode lasted a few weeks, at any rate in terms of where it was supposed to be heading at the beginning. After those few weeks, the Army took back control, and now the Muslim Brotherhood is fighting to gain the upper hand.

AB: What you just described is very similar to the "events" of May '68. They lasted for a few weeks, and then, as soon as the government was allowed to hold elections, the results were downright counter-revolutionary. We should never forget that, after May '68, the elections handed the Gaullist party a resounding victory. Faced with a choice between the movement and the state, as in Egypt (temporarily?), between the historic revolt and the Army, assisted by the Brotherhood, the elections – this is inevitable, in my view – will go in a conservative direction. However, in June 1968 you didn't draw the same skeptical conclusions about that sort of reversal as you're drawing now. On the contrary, you joined the Gauche Prolétarienne!

JCM: You can think the skepticism was there at the outset, but that's a retrospective diagnosis.

AB: No! I actually don't think it was there at the outset; I think it's the result of an assessment – the assessment of the tactical failure of the Maoism of that era.

JCM: It's very clear that when I joined a political organization, the Gauche Prolétarienne, I wasn't motivated by skepticism. But it was different when I left it. I'll leave my private reasons for doing so aside, even though they were the decisive factors. Let's just say that they made it impossible for me to overcome a skepticism I was already feeling. The Gauche Prolétarienne was seemingly flourishing at the time, and yet I had begun to be haunted by an uncanny feeling, prompted by the texts that were coming out of the Cultural Revolution then. I'm thinking in particular of a text denouncing the ideology of survival. It had struck me as portending the gravest dangers.

PP: *Your skepticism sometimes leads you to contend that all political discussion is pointless. What would your definition of politics be, then?*

JCM: My answer is very short. It boils down to what is for me the heart of the question of politics: the issue of bodies and their survival. That's ultimately the hard kernel. Indeed, a political discussion only becomes serious when it confronts that issue.

AB: We're finally hitting on an absolutely radical difference between us. The question of politics is of no interest to me whatsoever if it's exclusively a question of bodies and their survival – which is perfectly understandable, given that, in the end, we all die. It means that you'd have to acknowledge that, where politics is concerned, the criminal of criminals is Nature! When it comes to piling up corpses, Nature is second to none. That's moreover why, as Spinoza clearly saw, death and survival have only ever inspired moral or religious thinking. The real political issue has always been: what is the true life? This can also be expressed as, "What is a collective life under the sway of the Idea?" In the abstract, the question of the survival of bodies is related to the ominous concept of "biopolitics." Concretely, it's related to the general services of the state. In absolute contrast to all this, politics only has an existence if it can present itself as the actual becoming of an idea, as an idea's historical implementation. I'm not at all on the side of bodies and their survival but on the side of the real possibility that the collective body could actively share in a general idea of its becoming. The opposition between us is perfectly clear here.

The interesting thing about this opposition is that it ultimately provides two different assessments of the previous sequence. As Jean-Claude Milner was right to make clear, I can certainly not ascribe an original skepticism to him. I understand that his is a rigorous skepticism, the carefully considered, well thought-out, and anticipated consequence of a more general assessment of the revolutionary – or supposedly revolutionary – experience of 1968–71. What interests me is that at the end of what I've called the "second sequence," the basic debate could be expressed as follows: it's possible to say that what we did, with such passion, with such inspired, creative enthusiasm, was a failure. But since the question of failure, as we well know, is an ambiguous one, I ask: what was this supposed failure a failure *of*? Of one particular venture, such as, for example, French Maoism of the "Gauche Prolétarienne" type? Or of the general idea that underpinned and inspired that particular venture and a few others, which can be called "the beginning of the third stage of communism"? If your answer is that the failure was indeed that of the general idea, you plunge, as Milner has, into political skepticism. I think that, particularly from the 1980s on, that negative assessment has in fact prevailed.

We're still awash in political skepticism today. Everyone is well aware that everything that goes on – elections, "reforms," the politicians' overblown statements – is nothing but a cover for the most obdurate conservatism. No one expects any essential change, a new organization of society, and so on, to come out of it. But what we then realize is that skepticism is actually the ideology required for the continued existence of our states. It is what's demanded of people. The skeptical assessment has effectively led to a pragmatic embrace of things as they are. I'd even say: to the satisfaction people derive, in such a situation, from not having to lift a finger for an idea. Skepticism is also the blissful possibility, and even the supreme justification, for not having to be concerned about anything but yourself, since nothing can change the world as it is.

Then there's another assessment, a totally minority one, which is that what we experienced was the phase of transition between the second and third sequences of communism, in the sense of the three sequences I mentioned a moment ago. But if this is your assessment, it assumes that you admit that the opening of the third sequence may be a long, complex process. It should moreover be noted that there was a sizeable historical gap between the first stage of political Marxism, around 1840–50, and the completely unexpected success of Marxism-Leninism in 1917–20. As can easily be seen in the literature, political skepticism was absolutely dominant among the French intellectuals at the end of the nineteenth century, after the bloody failure of the Paris Commune. So, given such a historical gap, should political skepticism be promoted? I obviously don't think so. What should be promoted is an altogether unique, minority, and combative kind of tenacity, to restore the link between the Idea and the principle of organization in a figure that did not previously exist.

JCM: With regard to those whom Alain Badiou has called the "genuine intellectuals" (I'll leave the case of Sartre, which is a somewhat special one, aside), they themselves took stock of the experience. The most obvious case is that of Foucault. At first, he took extremely seriously the idea that survival is merely a question of ideology: that's what his texts on Iran and the Iranian revolution were about. But subsequently, in a way I can't analyze in him but which I can relate to, he repudiated those texts and ended up adopting a position of generalized skepticism.

I'd be tempted to paraphrase that itinerary as follows: "If the enterprise of the Gauche Prolétarienne in which I, Foucault, participated or which I at any rate supported, if the Iranian Revolution whose ideal was a substitute for it, if the end of the Cultural Revolution were all a train wreck; if this, that, or the other . . . well then (1) politics, fundamentally, is bricolage – and that takes me back to skepticism – and (2) the central question is indeed that of bodies and survival." Hence, the issue of biopolitics, which, in Foucault, is not just a gimmick: it means that the first and last word of politics is the *bios*, insofar as it stands opposed to the ever-present possibility of death. I think Alain Badiou's description is exactly right. May '68 plunged the figure of revolution into the present by wresting it away from the past of commemoration and the future of hope; whether that event was objectively revolutionary or not is another matter. The assessment of this experience of transition to the present amounted in the main to skepticism. And in the "best cases" – I'm putting scare quotes around that because I'm including myself in that group – a skepticism of the ancient type.

PP: *Which means what?*

JCM: Which means claiming that there's no method in politics, there are only data and facts, and in concrete situations you manage things as best you can, and for a very short, limited amount of time. I note that there's a sort of "postscript" in what Badiou said. Let me quote from memory: "It's the demand addressed by the dominant system for its own continued existence." But the two things need to be separated. First, there's the fact that a number of intellectuals experienced the possibility of revolution in the present. Then, after analyzing things, they concluded that what had presented itself to them as an experience of revolution in the present didn't conform to certain necessary markers of politics. And finally they generalized: "Skepticism is the horizon in which any political organizational discourse is inscribed." That process is one thing, but to say that it's a response to a political demand is something else again.

AB: That wasn't my thesis. I didn't say that political skepticism developed as a response to the state's demand. Naturally, I think that the movement of repudiation of a portion of the French intelligentsia, which was fully under way by the 1980s, was a renunciation and a dereliction of duty with respect to a historical task envisioned, namely, to close out Marxism-Leninism and invent the politics for the times ahead, however difficult a project that might be and however long it might take. But I'm not so scornful of that repudiation as to think that it was a response to the systemic demand of the bourgeois state. What I'm saying is that it was the expected subjective path by which that demand found its new form among the intellectuals, namely, political skepticism and the ethical concern for bodies and their survival. That combination is tailor-made, as we see all the time, for capitalo-parliamentarism, which is our societal form of state. So there was a congruence, but it wasn't the response to a demand; it was instead the development of a new form of the demand itself.

JCM: I don't find that convincing. There are two very different things involved. On the one hand, every established system – let's call it "governmental," if not "political" – seeks its own continued existence and issues an imprecise demand for discourses that can serve that continued existence. On the other hand, there are clear discourses and in particular those that the "genuine intellectuals" produce. Let's consider the period that's coming to an end as a result of the financial meltdown. It was linked to the assumption that the keys to continued prosperity had been found. These keys didn't function equally well, depending on what country was involved: France wasn't as good at it as Margaret Thatcher's England, which was a supposedly unsurpassable model, nor was it as good at it as Reagan's United States, which was also presented as an unsurpassable model, and so on. But, overall, everyone agreed, and when I say "everyone," I mean all those who were in one way or another part of a government machine: this was the case in Europe, in the United States, in Latin America, in Southeast Asia, in India, in Japan, in China, and so on. The premise was: "We know what continued, indefinite, and indefinitely increasing prosperity is." On that basis, the demand

addressed to the intellectuals in general was an imprecise one: "Produce the discourse for us that will best
suit this conviction." It so happened that in a number
of countries the discourse that best met the demand
was a form of skepticism. But, in the first place, it
wasn't to meet the demand that skepticism developed,
and in the second place, the intellectuals' skepticism,
or mine at any rate, didn't meet the demand for skepticism properly at all. The skepticism that was demanded
was not my kind of skepticism.

AB: But even your positive assertion suits the purpose
nonetheless, because as soon as one says that the question of politics boils down to the question of bodies
and their survival, one is naturally prepared to accept
the promise of general prosperity as the appropriate
promise. If the Idea has nothing to do with anything, if
the sole principle of politics is survival, then why not
crave the goods, including medicine, to make survival
pleasant and therefore desire above all the money with
which to obtain them? Because who is it that the promise
of continued prosperity appeals to? Well, first and foremost those who think that the question of politics boils
down to the question of bodies and their survival. Prosperity, of which capitalism and its lackeys claim to be
the only possible brokers, promises that all bodies will
be able to benefit from reasonable conditions of extended
survival. So there's a perfect fit between the doctrine
according to which what can and must be hoped for
concerns the survival of bodies and the general ideology
according to which, thanks to modern capitalism, we've
found the key to continued prosperity.

JCM: I don't think so at all. I think that the conviction
of having found the key to continued prosperity entails
the corollary that the question of the survival of bodies is
absolutely non-essential. Bodies and their survival, but
their non-survival as well, are only a means for continued

prosperity. Therefore, there's no correlation between them. It's possible to make them overlap. For example, in the United States, the promise of continued prosperity corresponded to the photo of the baby with the caption, "This baby will live to 100," and vice versa. But the fact that they overlap in some places or on some occasions in no way means that they're necessarily linked.

AB: As a promise, yes, they are. And what's more, it went hand in hand with all the propaganda hype about the humanitarian rescue operations, the images of which were shown (selectively, we should note, but that's another problem) everywhere: namely, some spot in the world where the survival of bodies wasn't guaranteed and where we consequently could – and had to – send in "humanitarian" paratroopers and tanks. That was the ideology of human rights, of humanitarian interventions, of the right of interference, a complete ideological system. Biopolitics was interpreted by the state from that angle. Why did it work? Why was there such wide support for it (because that support only crumbled as a result of the financial crisis)? The reason is that everyone – in the prosperous West – interpreted it to mean: "My survival, the survival of my body, has become the common interest of the political leaders who have found the key to universal prosperity." On a mass scale, nobody really cared that, behind all this, there were actually sordid statist-capitalist struggles going on over raw materials and energy sources. People weren't going to examine their fine moral consciences too closely; they were the quiet defenders of the survival of bodies and there was no need to bother about the Idea, imperialist machinations, the fate of peoples, communism, and all that sort of thing. Because the Idea disturbs the Western consumer's complacent political skepticism.

JCM: I completely acknowledge that a given individual might regard the promise of prosperity as the answer to his or her own belief that survival is the most important thing. But that doesn't mean, conversely, that the corollary of the promise of continued prosperity is the promise of survival. They're two different things; they're not symmetrical.

AB: Yes, but between the two are the politicians, the politicians in power, who serve precisely as interfaces. Their job is to say: the system – let's call it "capitalo-parliamentarian" – in its modern form has found the key to continued prosperity and I, the government in power, am the interface between this system of continued prosperity and the promise I make you that your bodies will be guaranteed good health and survival. The government's function is precisely that: to transmute one into the other. I'm not saying that it's a direct correspondence as regards capitalism itself, but as regards what governments, which are themselves immanent to generalized political skepticism, promise, that's really what happens.

JCM: Yes, but a government has no choice but to make a promise that will appeal to the people it needs to convince. Nothing implies that that promise has the slightest significance, however.

AB: That remains to be seen. Let's put ourselves in the broad framework of this system, the one in which you see the lackeys of the capitalist economy saying that it has found the key to continued prosperity and that it's the one and only system with the ability to find it. Let's consider the majority of people who are assumed to be concerned about the issue of survival and their own personal prosperity. Let's observe a government at work, announcing that it will match the system to people's desire, that it will be able to provide individuals with their most cherished version of the general economic prosperity promoted by capitalism, namely, their health, their personal well-being, their inner "harmony," and their indifference to everything that's not themselves. If, in such a context, someone were to say, as you do, that politics is only of interest when it's concerned about bodies and their survival, that someone would be strictly homogeneous to the context. They would then be its ideologue. The only thing that could be heterogeneous, in that case, would be an idea whose terrain of existence is not the survival of bodies, even if it's concerned about that.

JCM: They are homogenizable to all that, but homogenizable doesn't mean homogeneous. The system you're describing operates on the axiom "prosperity doesn't need bodies," it needs things, it arises from things. It's just that it can easily design its model, which doesn't need bodies, in such a way that it *promises* that it needs bodies. In that case, "homogenizable" means "heterogeneous."

AB: I think you're twisting the dialectic of identity and difference too hard here, because you've already excluded the role of states and political leaders, which are the operators by means of which the majority of people are won over to this system of promised prosperity. And they're won over because there's total homogeneity between government action and the system behind it. Now, the agents of capital that our political leaders have become, in a much more conspicuous and vital way than they were to Marx in the 1850s, are precisely those who subjectivate this homogeneity. They're the ones who can say, whatever the different versions of their discourses may be, that they're going to transform the eternal prosperity produced by capitalism into individualizable prosperity. It's abundantly clear that they do in fact do so to some extent, that some very difficult adjustments are made, that it's partly a lie, but in terms of subjectivity, that's the system as a whole; that's how it works. Can someone claim that they're heterogeneous to this system when they keep saying that the question of politics boils down to the question of the survival of bodies? I absolutely don't think so. And if that's the case, it's too homogenizable, really – to use your distinction between homogeneous and homogenizable.

JCM: It's too homogenizable to be really homogeneous.

AB: In any case, I haven't noticed that the capitalist system as a whole has found much to object to: it has even accommodated itself quite well – to humanitarianism in general, to the survival of bodies, to the propaganda of prosperity, and so on.

JCM: You can't seriously use that as an argument, because the very hallmark of this type of system is its ability to accommodate itself to everything.

PP: *This is a real point of contention. Let's pursue it further by introducing another idea, on the basis of your commentary, Jean-Claude Milner, on the Plague of Athens understood as a traumatic event. Let me quote a passage from* Clartés de tout *(2011): "The Plague of Athens wasn't an event for Plato; philosophy had no need to speak about it except to erase it, which is what Plato did in the* Symposium." *And later you say: "To make the Plague of Athens an unimportant event is a philosophical decision. To make it an important event and to make mortality the encounter of the unlimited universal rather than the encounter of the limited universal are, by contrast, radically anti-philosophical decisions. The possibility that that encounter might be related to the traumatic dimension of certain events is also anti-philosophical."[2] This is my question: it would seem that, for Alain Badiou, philosophy, but maybe politics too, must be continued, while, as far as you're concerned, Jean-Claude Milner, it must be rewritten, merely reconsidered. Because, in your view, there's no*

[2] *Clartés de tout* (Paris: Verdier, 2011), 49.

doubt that some traumatic experiences prevent the true life from being experienced immanently in every situation, as philosophers, in your opinion, would wish. Can you expand on that aspect?

JCM: I can only speak for myself. This intersects with the issue of Plato, which Alain Badiou has in a sense reactivated with his translation of the *Republic*.[3] I've always thought, and I don't think I'm wrong about this, that his relationship to Plato is constitutive of his discourse, whereas my non-relationship to Plato is also constitutive of my own discourse. This doesn't mean that I don't read the *Republic*, Badiou's translation of it in particular. In fact, I've always been struck by the contrast between Thucydides and Plato, a contrast that can be examined in detail.

I'll limit myself to the Plague of Athens. The extreme importance accorded it is very strange, if judged by modern criteria. Apparently, it wasn't a decisive event in the Peloponnesian War. There were much more important ones. But, for Thucydides, it *was* a decisive event. Plato, on the other hand, merely mentions it in passing, as something that happened and not much more. He doesn't pay a lot of attention to it.

I've always been struck by those contrasts. I devoted a considerable amount of thought to the subject and eventually arrived at the conclusion you summarized a moment ago. In effect, if one considers that the hard kernel of the minimalist politics I defend is the question of survival, then one ought to grant political relevance to every event in which the survival of the community is at stake, especially if that community has established itself as a community having a political existence. In the writings of Thucydides, Athens is the city par excellence, not necessarily the best one but the only one he

---

[3] See Alain Badiou, *Plato's Republic*, trans. Susan Spitzer (New York: Columbia University Press, 2013).

speaks about directly. Yet it's the Athenians who are hit by the plague and who, under its impact, will act like primitive people, without human or divine law.

In my opinion, events like these, these types of events, have political relevance structurally, precisely to the extent that they can make politics disappear. I can't speak for Alain Badiou, but when I read him it seems to me that the logic of his position ought to lead him to say that this type of event does not necessarily, structurally, have any political relevance. It may have some now and then, but not structurally.

AB: I'll grant you that without reservation. You perfectly pointed out the inherent consistency between, on the one hand, the idea that politics, in terms of its core, is centrally concerned with the problem of bodies and their survival and, on the other hand, the necessarily significant, even fundamental, character of traumatic events with respect to bodies and their survival. Ultimately, they amount to the same thing, but the first thesis, the one holding that the question of politics is the question of bodies and their survival, is clearly essential.

I obviously don't think that that's the core of politics. I think the core in reality is the historical process of the collective correlation between equality and freedom, or some such thing. Politics is the real of communism, in all its forms. Everything else is a matter of the state, of managing things.

Consequently, I think that traumatic events of natural origin, as is mainly the case with the plague, which was an epidemic event, or as with the famous Lisbon earthquake in the eighteenth century, can no doubt be important historically and have considerable political consequences. But no, I don't think they're political events properly speaking. Political thought is unable to take root in events like those. Besides, I can't see where any strong political thought ever began to establish itself constructively on the basis of disasters, other than to end up endorsing skepticism. In history, the meditation on disasters is of a theological or moral, never political, nature.

PP: *But the industrialized First World War, the veterans with severe facial injuries, the mass graves, the Second World War and the camps: doesn't all that mark a radical break?*

AB: That's something else. Wars and their consequences, as we well know, are within the sphere of politics but for reasons that are not commensurable with the decimation of bodies. That's unfortunately how it is. The reshuffling of the global balance of power that a war brings with it, as, for example, World War I as the sign of Europe's irreversible decline – a new stage and form of which, truth be told, we're seeing today – obviously has to do with the history of states and the history of politics. But the death toll can't be considered as the primary political fact. It's far more a consequence of politico-statist determinations, or a sort of symptom.

JCM: There's a fundamental difference of hierarchy between us, since I'd naturally be the first to be interested in the properly political aspects and dimension of events like World War I, which was between industrialized nations (1914), World War II, which was between industrialized nations (1939), or, prior to both of them, the American Civil War, which pitted the North, which was in the process of becoming an industrialized society, against the South, which rejected such a future, and so forth. I sometimes comment on these events from a political point of view, in the traditional sense of the term. But the fact is, in the hierarchy of my criteria, what leads politics to take into account not only shifts in countries' borders but infinitely more important shifts in terms of subjects is the issue of the massacres, the killing. And this is something we disagree about: Badiou doesn't deny the political import of mass graves, but it's secondary for him, whereas for me the relationship is reversed.

AB: I, for one, would say that the death toll, the corpses, the massacres are only intelligible in and of themselves – and that we can therefore only work to prevent them – if we understand the politics that made them possible. That's the order it works in. It's not in terms of massacres as such that politics can be thought; it's in terms of politics that massacres need to be thought. It's clear that the Nazi genocide of the Jews is a historical fact of the utmost importance, but I think that the root of its intelligibility – namely, understanding what created the possibility for such a massacre – can only be found by understanding Nazi politics *qua* politics. And Nazi politics can't be reduced to that alone: it included all sorts of aspects and it placed that horror within its self-representation as a whole. So, it's not that I'm not interested in massacres, absolutely not, but I think that the understanding of massacres, and therefore the possibility that they won't recur, forces you to come back to the understanding of politics properly speaking, that is – let's face it – to what the Nazis' ideas were. I say "idea" because, unfortunately, "idea" in itself doesn't have a positive meaning. Some political ideas are criminal.

PP: *You both answered in terms of politics, but you didn't use the distinction that was drawn between philosophy and anti-philosophy in one of Jean-Claude Milner's sentences that I quoted above. How does the issue of survival and trauma intersect with that of the rift between philosophy and anti-philosophy?*

JCM: Just to clarify things, it's obvious that our disagreement has to do with a hierarchy between what's primary and what's secondary in importance. Neither of us thinks that what's secondary in his own framework is unimportant. In other words, I'd allow that Alain Badiou is not indifferent to mass murder, and, likewise, he'd allow that I'm not indifferent to political determinations – and in particular to Nazi ideas, which I've also studied. There is, in fact, a flip side to what I'm saying. Roughly speaking, I'd say: philosophy is Plato; that is, the hypothesis that the idea of politics is primary. I'm taking politics in its broadest sense. In Plato, it's the idea of the City; in Badiou, it's the idea of revolution or the communist hypothesis, which includes the idea of politics in the Platonic sense. The fact that the idea of politics is the primary element and that everything that's different from it is necessarily secondary seems to me to be a fundamentally philosophical position. This is the position that Alain Badiou has presented as his own, and it also seems to me to characterize the position I think I perceive in Plato. Conversely, my position is not just anti-political – if "political" is defined as Badiou defines it, whereas if "political" is defined as I define it, my position is, on the contrary, eminently political – but most certainly anti-philosophical, or at any rate if philosophy is defined as I define it and as Alain Badiou, I think, defines it.

AB: Your description seems spot on to me. But let's not forget, amid the complex layers of the discussion, that what I regard as the rigorous and unavoidable consequence of the position that makes the idea secondary to the real or historical character of the abuse of bodies inevitably leads to political skepticism. We shouldn't lose sight of that, because, in this regard, I think that Jean-Claude Milner is logically coherent within the field he describes, as compared with others who purport to maintain a phantom, a specter, of genuine, ideal, etc. politics.

In actual fact, we have two distinct frameworks: one that maintains the possibility of politics as the organized realization of an idea, an idea that may vary, and one that, on the basis of traumatic events that may have afflicted bodies and their survival and might do so again, leads to favoring bricolage in politics. Those are the two positions. So it's important to see that the price paid for promoting traumatic events as a starting point – I'm not saying all the rest is disregarded – is that, since no idea can be commensurable with such trauma, the reparative bricolage of a pragmatics of state ends up being what can best be trusted. And once that's been said, we're not involved in a discussion about politics anymore.

I think that, all things considered, Jean-Claude Milner shouldn't contrast the reality of politics with the possibly fatal fiction of philosophy but should instead formulate clearly his position, which is that politics doesn't exist. It doesn't exist because what exist are reparative and protective opportunities with regard to bodies and their survival. I can't see why the action that might be taken to prevent or prohibit mass murder should be called "politics." It's really a matter of a pragmatics, whether organized or unorganized, statist, personal, or collective: the pragmatics of the defense of the integrity of bodies. And such a pragmatics of the integrity of bodies is obviously related to an ethical or moral concern, a sort of generalized therapeutics, which has no reason to seize upon the word "politics."

JCM: We can quibble about words, but why do I still have a soft spot for the word "politics"? First of all, because to my ear it sounds like a pun, that is, I spell "politics" in two different ways – *poli* with an *i*, on the one hand, and *poly* with a *y*, on the other hand. I mean, the question of politics basically rests on the fact that there are many speaking bodies. As soon as there are many speaking beings, each can prevent each of the others from speaking; it reduces the other to the state of a non-speaking being, i.e., of a speaking non-being or a thing. That sounds like a Hegelian thesis, but with one difference – and it's a big one. In Hegel, the game involves two, and the two is crucial; here, the many constitutes an open, unlimited series, which, in any case, begins with more than two. This is why the question of the plurality of speaking beings is the minimum core of the question of politics for me. I'll admit that the term "politics" is being used in an unconventional way, but I have a number of reasons for using it that way.

PP: *In your opinion, Alain Badiou, is this politics of speaking beings anti-philosophical?*

AB: I wouldn't immediately regard it as anti-philosophical, first of all because it's a definition of politics and, as a definition of politics, it has to be examined from the point of view of politics. But the point is, I think Jean-Claude Milner, Jean-Claude Milner's unique body of work, invigorates his political skepticism with the force given it by Lacan's anti-philosophy. He does so on the basis of the fact that he suspects philosophy of not really taking into account the threat constantly hanging over speaking beings, the threat that one of them might prevent the others from speaking – meaning that philosophy supposedly doesn't take the question of the tyrant into account. That's pretty odd, moreover, since Plato, the quintessential philosopher, is also the first to have inscribed the subjective figure of the tyrant into the discourse of philosophy and the first to have described him in great detail, even in terms of the unconscious motives he's driven by. Can it be that a defender of anti-philosophy sometimes doesn't even realize that he's up to his eyeballs in philosophy? Whatever the case may be, anti-philosophy, in this regard, results from the suspicion it casts on philosophy insofar as philosophy ignores the speaking body and approaches things from the perspective of the Idea.

PP: *From the perspective of the Idea or of the discourse of the master?*

AB: Yes, perhaps. Everyone knows masters are needed in philosophy, and that doesn't bother me in the least. At any rate, if it's a question of the view it has of politics, the fact is that philosophy in general, and my philosophy absolutely, refuses to be predicated purely and simply on the multiplicity of speaking bodies. As far as I'm concerned, I'd just point out – in any case as regards the view I have of it – that I begin with multiplicity. Does that multiplicity necessarily have to be one of bodies? That's the whole question. For example, does the multiplicity of subjects mean the multiplicity of speaking bodies?

In other words, the debate could be as follows: is "speaking bodies" an adequate enough definition of the dwelling space of human communities to allow us to immediately speak about politics? I don't think so. I think that it is the initial determination of human beings as reducible to the multiplicity of speaking bodies that already prevents our speaking about politics, because politics presupposes many other parameters in the very definition of the subject in question than just the fact that he or she is a speaking body.

The speaking body only defines humanity in general. But politics doesn't deal with humanity in general; politics is something that presupposes the figure of the state, a system of relations between subjects that aren't reducible to their mere survival, and, in addition, events that are the condition for a specific type of truth. What's more, this approach can already be found to some extent in what Jean-Claude Milner said, because if one speaking body can prevent other speaking bodies from speaking, it is necessarily for reasons that aren't deducible from the fact that they're speaking bodies. But what are those reasons, then? That's where politics begins, just barely.

JCM: And that's where our disagreement begins! Since I think that prohibiting – I prefer to say preventing – is not just the necessary but the sufficient condition for there to be politics.

AB: Because you confuse "politics," which is a thought-practice, and "state," which is a power-institution, and that's the crucial mistake in this domain. However, my question didn't have to do with that issue. It had to do with the very notion of preventing. You can't deduce the notion of preventing from the mere fact that a multiplicity of speaking bodies is involved. Preventing assumes a very complex regulation of relationship among speaking bodies, which you can't deduce from the mere fact that they're speaking bodies.

JCM: I think we disagree completely on this issue. I think that the existence of speech alone is in itself a preventing.

AB: So then preventing is unavoidable.

JCM: Yes, absolutely.

AB: So if preventing is unavoidable, how can it be prevented?

JCM: Because it can be ruled, it can be regulated.

AB: If it can be regulated, that means it can be prevented. You can clearly see that you're necessarily introducing a dialectic different from that of mere identity/difference between speaking bodies. No political consideration whatsoever can be deduced from the mere multiplicity of speaking bodies because, in actual fact, we're dealing with regulations of prohibition, of preventing prohibition, or of prohibiting preventing, and you can't deduce these regulations from the mere multiplicity of speaking bodies.

JCM: The debate we've gotten into is almost like a return to the model of the post-Kantian disputes. I'll grant that this isn't hypothetico-deductive, but let's regard these as sequential theses. The first thesis is the multiplicity of speaking bodies; the second thesis is that a speaking body, merely by existing, prevents any other speaking body from acting as a speaking body; the third thesis is that either we leave it at that and there are no more speaking bodies, or else speaking bodies continue to be speaking bodies and this assumes that there's a system of regulation, that is, of a succession of *prises de parole*, and so forth. So, let's say this chain of propositions isn't hypthetico-deductible . . .

AB: But the integration of the various levels isn't. The transition from the first to the second level is already strictly unintelligible. Why should it be inferred in any way from the multiplicity of speaking bodies that a speaking body can prohibit the others from speaking?

PP: *Which amounts to questioning how the preventing would be constitutive?*

AB: Precisely. You could just as well say, on the contrary, that speech is in itself the permission given to the other person to answer a question. Or even an elicitation of the other's speech. It's really quite dogmatic to think that the second level is constituted the way you say, and, as for the transition from the second to the third, it's totally unintelligible, because if it's in the power of any speaking body to prevent the others from speaking, and if that's what happens automatically, it's hard to see where regulation would come from. It would have to be inscribed, in an ex-centered way, in the situation itself. Lacan called that ex-centered inscription the Other. I call it the state

– in a very general way, incidentally: the state of the situation.

PP: *Could this notion of preventing be made clearer with the notion of power?*

JCM: As far as I'm concerned, it's the mere fact of existence itself, of the *prise de parole* itself. Granted, this may be obvious only to me, but in the way that the *cogito* is obvious only to the person expressing it. It doesn't bother me when people tell me: "It's not demonstrable, it's not deducible, they're only assertions."

AB: Well, it bothers me that it doesn't bother you. But, in addition, the problem isn't simply that it's non-deducible; what I think is that it's intrinsically unintelligible. To be functional and comprehensible, your model would have to assume that in reality what there is – the "there is" as such – is always made up (let's take your axiomatics) of speaking bodies in a field where a kind of regulation is operative. And, for you, that's what politics – or what amounts to the same thing, its factual non-existence – is. This is the most abstract definition possible of the fact that there's always a power, a state of the situation, of speaking bodies. I'm willing to accept the situation being reduced to multiplicity – besides, multiplicity is my chief onto-logical category – but I think you should accept that that multiplicity (in your view of things, that of speaking bodies) is always subject to regulations of prohibition or authorization that are immanent to its field of existence.

PP: *Jean-Claude Milner, isn't your argument really about speaking bodies insofar as they are always captured in modes of discourse, in power and knowledge*

*relationships? For example, when René Cassin[4] decided
to replace the word "international" with the word
"universal" in 1948, he prevented those who wanted
to preserve the word "international" from speaking.
Doesn't a declaration of that sort moreover – like the
one in 1789 – help illustrate your point?*

JCM: It's possible to use that sort of illustration. What
I fully accept as an objection or a flat rejection of my
method is that it's deliberately abstract. It *is* a deliberately abstract genealogy.

AB: That's the level at which I'm trying to understand it.

JCM: As far as I'm concerned, it's a sequential process.
What I mean by that is that, at first, there's not
necessarily what seems essential in Alain Badiou's critique, namely, the idea that as soon as there's a multiplicity there's a possibility of regulation in an immanent
way. Not for me there isn't. As far as I'm concerned,
these are sequential stages.

AB: As soon as there are multiplicities, if you want to
make intelligible the fact that one element of the multiplicity is in a position to prevent the others in that multiplicity from existing in the same way as it does – which
for you means to prohibit them from speaking, for
example – then you assume there's something more in
the powers a given speaking multiplicity has than what
it's originally assumed to have as a simple multiplicity.
Because that power, of prohibiting or preventing, is a relation. So in your genealogy you also have to think relation.

---

[4] René Cassin (1887–1976), a French jurist, law professor, and judge,
received the Nobel Peace Prize in 1968 for his work in drafting the
Universal Declaration of Human Rights, adopted by the United
Nations General Assembly in 1948.

Yet you don't think that the body is a relation, but neither is speech one, since, for you, the *prise de parole* always amounts to prohibiting the other from speaking.

JCM: Absolutely.

AB: But that's precisely what doesn't make sense. First of all, I can't see any reason why the *prise de parole* should be equivalent to prohibiting the other from speaking.

JCM: Because it's not a relation.

AB: But if neither the body nor speech is a relation, and if there are only speaking bodies, then is there no hope of there ever being any regulation? Because only a relation can be regulated; nothing else can. If there are only speaking beings, you can't regulate either the fact that they're bodies or the fact that they speak, since that's their very definition. So if you can't regulate any of the terms, what *can* you regulate? You've got to be able to regulate a relation . . .

JCM: I don't agree: the first relation is a regulation.

AB: I quite agree, but what does it regulate?

JCM: It only regulates coexistence and co-presence.

AB: But it has to regulate something a lot more specific! It has to regulate the possibility for the *prise de parole* to no longer be a prohibition of the others from speaking! Now, I'm sorry, but that assumes there's a relation. I can't see how you can do away with relation and then regulate it.

JCM: Well, now I'm the one who doesn't understand. What do you mean by "assume"?

AB: You assume that what exists is a multiplicity of speaking bodies and you further assume that any *prise de parole* prohibits the others from speaking. That's what I take "assumption" to mean.

JCM: I understand. Given the multiplicity of speaking bodies, Alain Badiou posits that the potential for regulation is already included in it. But I don't see any necessary link between those two moments.

AB: Not just potentially, in actual fact! It's odd: in a certain way you're bringing back Rousseau's hypothesis about a state of nature.

JCM: Yes.

AB: That's exactly what it is. And then comes the social contract. I thought you were very anti-Rousseauist with respect to this issue, so it's a bit of a surprise for me. Do you really assume that there's a state of nature and that, at a given moment – which has always been a mysterious element in Rousseau's genealogy, assuming the intervention of a lawgiver from who knows where – this state of natural dispersion becomes a dense relational state?

JCM: I admit that I assume something similar to a state of nature, but the fact remains that, rather than positing isolation and dispersion, I posit co-presence, and it's this co-presence that will be the problem. Yes, I'm a Rousseauist, as far as a position of a state of nature, or in any case an initial logical time, is concerned, but I'm not one, as far as the *structure* of that state of nature is concerned. Instead of Rousseau, you could cite the Freud of *Totem and Taboo* (1913).

AB: Right, all genealogies of that sort, all the genealogies that presuppose that there's a non-relational state of co-presence – whereas a relation is always already there. As soon as a multiple is localized, and it always is, there is a relation.

PP: *Could you be more specific about your differences regarding this state of co-presence?*

JCM: In fact, my position is pretty simple and banal. It's what everyone thinks.

PP: *Meaning?*

JCM: It's what Freud thinks, so it's what everyone thinks!

AB: *I* claim that it's not what you yourself think! Nobody thinks that a relation, regulation by the state, are things that suddenly appear incomprehensibly in a world of pure co-presence where everyone moreover prevents the other person from existing!

JCM: I think I've made my position clear, whether it's accepted or not. I think I understand your criticisms; what I'd like is for you to put something forward.

AB: But wherever there's speech, there's something of the big Other, that's all. So wherever there's speech, there's already a relational regulation of that speech.

JCM: Yes, with Badiou the focal point is the "already," whereas with me it's a "not yet." When the multiplicity of speaking beings first appears, there's not yet any relational regulation of their speech, in my view.

AB: OK. To clarify things, I'd say that, for me, generally speaking, when multiplicity appears it's always already in a transcendental form that organizes the system of possible relations.

JCM: I'm glad to hear you say that, because that's what I thought you think. I think that your framework is based on an "always/already," which is a sort of basic operator. I'm using that expression because it's familiar.

AB: I think it's as if your conception was actually atomistic.

JCM: I was going to say as much. And "my" philosopher, I dare say, is Lucretius.

AB: But with Lucretius there was already the *clinamen*.

JCM: So it's Lucretius without the *clinamen*!

AB: I'm glad to hear you say so, because Lucretius without the *clinamen*, from Lucretius' own point of view, ultimately leads to the fact that nothing is regulated, nothing happens.

JCM: There's no nature, right.

AB: I'm struck once again by the fact that, right from the start, a sort of instantaneous split has been occurring between us on the basis of one point that, although almost invisible, we share and is always the same. This point that the two of us have in common is a very meager matrix, which can be expressed as: there is multiplicity, pure coexistence. For me, it's in the ontological figure of set theory, in which a relation does not in fact exist (it is itself a form of the multiple). And for you, it's the coexisting multiplicity of speaking bodies, without even the *clinamen*. That's the matrix.

But then a difference of opinion instantly arises. Jean-Claude Milner's construct operates by means of an enigmatic transition to "another level," since there's no "already" that can constitute a relation, while for me – this is the transition from *Being and Event* to *Logics of*

Worlds – if that were true, it would be the way it is in Lucretius without the *clinamen*: nothing would ever have happened, except for atoms. In order for there to be something, what I call a "world" and what Milner calls a "nature," you have to assume that the coexisting multiples are identified and differentiated by relational conditions that I term "the transcendental of the world." Basically, Jean-Claude Milner remains in a radical atomistics, and, in the final analysis, hypothesizes that it's only with relations that are always circumstantial and cobbled together, always ultimately more or less non-existent, that the prohibitions that any atom (any speaking body) constitutes for all the others can be prevented. For Milner, there's no general relation, nor is there any general doctrine of any of this. There's no world.

JCM: That's right, there's no nature in the singular, as far as I'm concerned; there's no world. So, yes, the dichotomy between our approaches is blatantly obvious.

PP: *There's no nature but there's intrinsic human solitude!*

JCM: I'm not sure that's the word I'd use. I think the word "atomism" is better, including in terms of indivisibility, since that's my theory of bodily freedoms, i.e., that there's an impenetrable core, if only with regard to the most basic functions of the police. A regime of freedom can be identified, among other features, by the fact that, when confronted with the police, a speaking being endowed with a body has the ability to put up a barrier that no legal power has the right to cross. In the "politics of things,"[5] the whole problem comes down to

---

[5] Very roughly, Milner's concept of "the politics of things" describes an increasingly threatening state of affairs in which speaking beings, governed by things – polls and markets, for example – whose intentions are interpreted by so-called "experts," are ultimately transformed into inert things themselves.

regarding subjects as impenetrable, whereas things are penetrable . . .

AB: . . . are always penetrable, and that's an issue with which I'm descriptively completely in agreement. What's more, it's a crucial issue today.

JCM: That's why I don't like the word "solitude."

AB: As for me, "solitude" would only be meaningful in the generic element of the construction of a truth. In the generic element of the construction of a truth it is usually a question of a number of individuals, or communities, or even a universal sensibility. Consequently, remaining outside such a construction can instigate a feeling of solitude. To be alone is always to be excluded from a truth that can be shared. It would make sense for me to speak of solitude in love, when you've lost the other person. Another terrible example of the experience of solitude would be not to be able to understand the proof of a theorem, or to stand there indifferently on the sidewalk when a revolutionary demonstration is taking place. Or to listen uncomprehendingly to the first performance of a work of music that will later be regarded as a masterpiece. Thus, solitude can come about to the extent that truths are created. It's not a primordial given.

2

Considerations on Revolution, Law, and Mathematics

PP: *You mentioned your involvement in the "Red Years" and your relationship to China. In retrospect, what is your assessment of those years and the Cultural Revolution? Today, after Simon Leys's books and Wang Bing's films about China, and Rithy Panh's films, as well as François Bizot's books, about Cambodia,[1] what do you think about the long-suppressed memory of the Cultural Revolution and the massacres committed in Cambodia in the name of the Revolution?*

[1] Simon Leys's many books about China include *The Chairman's New Clothes* (1981), *Chinese Shadows* (1977), and *Broken Images* (1979). Among the director Wang Bing's eight films are the prize-winning, nine-hour-long documentary *Tie Xi Qu: West of the Tracks* (2003), *Feng Ming: A Chinese Memoir* (2007), and *Crude Oil* (2008). Rithy Panh has made several films about Cambodia, including *Between War and Peace* (1991), *Rice People* (1994), *Bothana* (1996), and *S-21: The Khmer Rouge Killing Machine* (2003). His latest film, *The Missing Picture*, was awarded a prize at the 2013 Cannes Film Festival. François Bizot, a French survivor of Khmer Rouge captivity, wrote about his experience in *The Gate* (2004) and *Facing the Torturer* (2012).

JCM: "Suppression" is not the word I'd use where I'm concerned. I read Simon Leys's *The Chairman's New Clothes* very early on. What I can say is that I filtered it through the revolution or at least through one of its models, the predominant model back then. The book can be summarized as follows. The sequence that began in 1789 and continued through 1793 defined the horizon of everything that later adopted the name "revolution." But if every revolution's paradigm is the French Revolution, then, in effect, it will be accompanied by killings. The fact that there were killings in China was therefore neither surprising nor a decisive factor for me.

What I realized later was that the Cultural Revolution had to be viewed as something altogether unique. In fact, it brought the model of revolution that had influenced me, which I just mentioned, to an end. The Chinese revolution of 1949 was still part of that model, but the Cultural Revolution wasn't. When I belonged to the Maoist movement, I had the increasingly strong feeling that everything about the "Great Proletarian Cultural Revolution" – that was the name it adopted – had to be taken seriously: it was great as compared with earlier revolutions; it was great because it was proletarian, while the previous ones hadn't been, for historical reasons where the French Revolution was concerned and for reasons having to do with "blunders" or "failures" where the Soviet Revolution was concerned. Finally, it was great and proletarian because it was cultural. It wasn't limited to production relations or to revolutionary war but extended to culture as a whole. In fact, it attacked the very possibility of culture. The Cultural Revolution wasn't the secondary consequence of the achieved revolution but the very condition of that achievement. It was a radical innovation within the model and it no doubt forced the model to be abandoned.

Once I realized that, the issue of killings became increasingly important. At our last meeting I mentioned the importance that the issue of the philosophy of survival had taken on for me at that time. All the information that came later confirmed my feeling that something very unusual was going on. And I had this feeling while I was still a militant in the Gauche Prolétarienne. Naturally, I wouldn't say that, at the time, I understood the full extent of what was going on. Nevertheless, I wouldn't say that what I learned about Cambodia (information about Cambodia came through pretty early on) or what I'm still learning today about China (the many accounts of the Cultural Revolution have appeared gradually over time) led to my break with Maoism. The break had occurred before, first in the guise of the radical novelty that I attributed to the Cultural Revolution and later with the realization that this novelty had become repellent to me.

AB: My view of things is obviously totally different. First of all, I want to underscore the fact that, just as the most extreme violence has always accompanied revolutionary phenomena, starting with the paradigm of the French Revolution and extending right up to the Cultural Revolution doubtless as the final figure – I'll come back to this – of the paradigm of revolution, so the reduction of revolutionary phenomena to massacres accompanies, goes hand in hand with, and is even constitutive of counter-revolutionary propaganda. You could even say that the overall framework of such counter-revolutionary propaganda was in place by 1815 or so, when Robespierre was presented no differently from the way Pol Pot is presented today, namely, as a murderous lunatic spreading unlimited violence, which doomed the phenomenon of revolution at its very core. So, when one is subjectively on the side of the tradition of revolutions, of the idea of revolution, a natural distrust of anything resembling that more than 200-year-old propaganda is essential.

Let's go back to the years 1960–70. We were aware of all this, and we were revolutionaries. So we regarded the issue of violence very differently. Revolutionary violence was accepted as the inherent condition of the revolutionary tradition in various forms, including, as is well known, a very complex relationship between what could be called legal or semi-legal violence (the Revolutionary Tribunals of the Republic, the executions, the military repression of the rebellion in the Vendée) and the numerous local massacres occurring in a context of popular terror. Its paradigm was right from the start the massacres of September 1792 in the case of the French Revolution, as opposed, precisely, to the politically controlled action of the Revolutionary Tribunals.

There has always been a combination of extreme state violence and mass terrorist violence in revolutions, and revolutionaries, people with a revolutionary subjectivity, have always acknowledged that this was the case. Likewise, counter-revolutionary propaganda has always maintained that the essence of revolutions was ultimately criminal in nature. If I think back to the period in question, bearing all this in mind, it must be said that the issue of violence was by no means central to our political concerns. The focus of our questions was: what are we dealing with, from the standpoint of politics? What result are we aiming for? What kind of transformation of society is involved? It was on the basis of the answers to these questions that we judged violence; it was not on the basis of violence that we judged the answers.

As far as the Cultural Revolution was concerned, we were indeed faced with an unprecedented and unique figure of the paradigm, in terms of its size and the length of time it lasted, but above all in terms of the fact that this revolutionary phenomenon was occurring in the context of a *socialist* state. That, for us, was the key point, which defined the opposition between Maoism and Stalinism.

Stalinism exercised a quasi-unlimited reign of police, centralized, and state terror. The Chinese state inherited that terror to a great extent for years, but with the Cultural Revolution something unique and irreducible occurred: a revolution in the context of a socialist state. How did we experience it at the time? We experienced it as a new chance being given the paradigm of mass revolution after its takeover by the Stalinist state. So the Cultural Revolution naturally seemed to be reopening the horizon of revolution in conditions that were those of a socialist state. That's why I've always said that, in a way, the Cultural Revolution, in an utterly different context, played the same strategic role with respect to thought as the Paris Commune had played in the nineteenth century. The Paris Commune had been the first form – as we used to say back then – of the dictatorship of the proletariat. It had been the first temporarily victorious communist and workers' insurrection. However, it ultimately failed; it was crushed in bloodshed. The Cultural Revolution was the first attempt at a communist revolution within a socialist state. So there was a unique and originary aspect to each of these revolutions, which in fact led to an internal comparison, because reference to the Paris Commune very quickly became an explicit component of the Chinese revolutionaries' subjectivity.

The fundamental issue, as I see it, is not so much the fact that we know the extent and details of the killings, as often happens after periods of revolution. The key point is that the Cultural Revolution was a total failure. And just as after the collapse of the Paris Commune, which, for Marx and later for Lenin, led to a fundamental revision of communist political thought, we should examine closely, after the failure of the Cultural Revolution, not only the Cultural Revolution itself, the ultra-leftist terrorism of Cambodia, and so forth, but ultimately the very category of "revolution." Not because it was accompanied by great violence throughout its history, but because it's conceivable today, when it's a question of this unique type of revolution endeavoring to establish a communist, as opposed to a democratic or republican, order, that the category of "revolution" has perhaps exhausted its usefulness for thought and political subjectivity.

PP: *Can a link be established between the ideas of the exhaustion of revolution and the exhaustion of history? I can put the question more prosaically: can we say, for example, that the historical interpretation of the Commune is still an issue today? There is, of course, the book by Pierre Dardot and Christian Laval (*Marx, prénom: Karl*), which reopened the question in a substantial chapter in which the authors discuss how little attention Marx paid to the Communards' ideas. The anniversary of the Commune is still an issue of remembrance, as was clear in the 2012 French presidential election. But can we seriously say that the Commune is still a political issue?*

AB: The primary issue today, in my view, is the assessment of the Cultural Revolution, which we have witnessed in our lifetime. And it's only as a result of such an assessment – the question of what the Cultural Revolution was all about – that we can reconsider the assessment of the Paris Commune, as the Cultural Revolution itself in fact did. Why is this so? Because the underlying question is that of communism.

The Paris Commune was a revolution that opened up the possibility of revolutions that aren't reducible to republican or democratic ideas but instead have loftier ideals and, in addition, convey the political significance of the word "worker." There was indeed a cycle that went from the Paris Commune to the Cultural Revolution, of that I'm sure. The Cultural Revolution starkly posed the question – since the context was already that of the socialist state – of what a revolution was whose general orientation, guiding principle, and watchwords propelled the historical movement toward communism, not in its statist, stabilized form but in terms of the mass movement itself.

The question opened by that revolution was: what is a communist mass movement? To be convinced of this, we need only recall some of the Cultural Revolution's basic watchwords: to put an end to the division between intellectual and manual labor; to put an end to the traditional forms of the division of labor; to completely overhaul the issue of gender equality; to redistribute political power in the form of local revolutionary committees; to create a truly egalitarian education, and so forth. All of this could, moreover, be claimed by the Paris Commune as well. But, in my view, the issue we need to think about now is the relationship between revolution and communism.

The Cultural Revolution can be regarded as the first attempt to create a genuine communist politics on a mass scale. And this attempt should be distinguished from all the ones that presented themselves as "proletarian revolutions," the classic example being that of October 1917: revolutions that built new kinds of dictatorial popular states, which called themselves socialist states. Note that they didn't call themselves communist states. "Communist state" is an oxymoron, since communism is geared toward the withering away of the state. They called themselves socialist states. Thus, in 1917, we witnessed the birth of a paradigm of revolutions and socialist states. The Cultural Revolution couldn't be a "socialist" revolution, however, since it was a revolution within – and largely against – a socialist state, and it occurred under the banner of communism.

So, to return to the original question, we can say that the tradition of revolutionary violence, as the destruction of the previous figure of the state and the construction of a new type of state, seems to have been shown to be unsuitable, for reasons that are still partly unclear, for what can be called the communist movement as such. It may be that "communist revolution" is not just an oxymoron but one that signals the end of any creative use of the word "revolution."

JCM: There's clearly one point we agree on and one we disagree on. The one we agree on concerning the Cultural Revolution is its aspect of closure. Even if the notion of closure itself contains the seed of a subsidiary disagreement – does the closure remain within what it closes or does it already start being external to it? – we're still in agreement overall. The point we disagree on has to do very specifically with the issue of killing.

Let's clear the ground. Alain Badiou summarized the line of argument adopted back then by those he calls "subjects with a revolutionary sensibility": the notion of violence is inherent in revolution, and the fact that this violence is shocking and outrageous is also inherent in the very notion of revolutionary violence. I have no objection to this way of presenting things. I recognize myself in it the way I was back then. When it comes to me, though, there's a difference – I'm bringing this up again for the sake of clarity. Once I had the feeling that the Cultural Revolution was bringing the model of revolution as it had functioned for most of the *gauchistes* in France (and for many other people in France and elsewhere) to an end, I sensed that it was also changing the status of killing. In other words, there was a before and after the Cultural Revolution.

The earlier model had made it possible to deal with a number of problems relating to killings – not in terms of a "globally positive"[2] balance sheet; that's not the point. The crucial point is that, in revolutionary conflict, as in any conflict moreover, there is a dimension of killing. Now, unlike conventional warfare, in which

[2]In 1982 Georges Marchais, the head of the French Communist Party, described the achievements of the Soviet Union and its Eastern European allies as "globally positive."

the legitimacy of the state-form is automatically accepted, revolutionary warfare challenges the state-form – and, through it, all existing forms of legality. Consequently, acts of violence in a revolution take on a distinctive character in that they are always necessarily inscribed in the horizon of illegality. To criticize them for their illegality is to reject the very notion of revolution. So far, so good. But as soon as I realized that the Proletarian Cultural Revolution was drastically changing the previous frame of interpretation, it also meant that the previous way of dealing with killings was no longer valid. When the issue of survival is made a matter of pure and simple ideology, then the question of killing in all its starkness must be taken into account.

Today – this wouldn't have been the case in the 1970s, though – I would go so far as to focus on the notion of culture, which is implied in the name "Cultural Revolution." Such a revolution must begin by destroying all pre-existing forms of culture. Fine. But so as to construct a different one or to dispense with culture altogether? That's an open question. At any rate, what is a culture in general if not a regulation of killing and survival? To consider the issue of killing and survival a matter of ideology is to suspend all regulation of killing. That may be an area of disagreement between us. In any case, I wanted to clarify this.

Of course, one of the basic facts we need to keep in mind today is that the Cultural Revolution was a failure. On many levels: it was an internal failure because it's not true – to borrow that quip of Brecht's – that you can dissolve a people and replace it with another, and it's not true that to implement a social model of any sort a people can massacre itself in the name of the people in order to put another people, as it were, in its place. That amounts to a failure inscribed in the very terms of the project. Then there's a second reason, which is that it has to be judged by its consequences. What I mean by this is that the Great Proletarian Cultural Revolution wiped itself out. By dint of destroying all the traditional forms of Chinese history it destroyed itself as a historical phase.

To borrow an argument that Alain Badiou used against me, even though I don't accept it as far as I myself am concerned, I'd say that the Cultural Revolution did everything that needed to be done for capitalism to be instituted in China. Everything that had to do with a tradition of distrust vis-à-vis capitalistic forms in China was eliminated. The possibility of driving the peasants off their land, as is currently happening before our very eyes, was one of the possibilities opened up by the Proletarian Cultural Revolution.

For me, failure is a standard of judgment. Given that the notion of success is an unclear and muddled one, successful revolutions have been few and far between. The French Revolution accomplished something. I'm not saying it did so in the way it intended, but it did accomplish something: even today, the status of land ownership in France bears the traces of the nationalization of the clergy's property. You can appreciate how important a decision that was when you look at a country like Greece, where the Orthodox Church owns much of the land and no one dares mention that one way of resolving Greece's economic problems might be to nationalize the clergy's property. The revolutions that have succeeded by achieving part of their objectives are not as common as all that. I have no respect for the ones that failed. I'm one of those – let me say this very clearly – who don't have a lot of respect for the Commune, because it was defeated.

AB: If, in effect, there were an abundance or an overabundance of victorious revolutions, we'd know about it. The scarcity of revolutionary victories is a well-established fact, and that's why we can consider that we're still in prehistory, to use Marx's vocabulary, and even in a particularly regressive phase of prehistory, today.

Don't forget that the revolutionary sequence we're talking about, which began with the French Revolution and continued with the Paris Commune, the Soviet Revolution, and the Chinese Revolution, is an extremely short historical period. It's just two little centuries – in other words, nothing at all, compared with the thousands of years that the many different kinds of state-forms and the most ruthless class divisions have lasted. We've got to look a little further ahead and not imagine, as Fukuyama does, that a few centuries of capitalist expansion, a few decades of a truly global market, amount to the end of History. The history of humanity relieved of the heaviest burdens of its underlying animality, i.e., the history of communism, is only just beginning!

But there's a point I'd like to go back to. First of all, I don't think that the issue of the Cultural Revolution's indubitable failure passes any judgment on the internal relationship between failure and terror, because the French Revolution, insofar as it was partly victorious, literally invented terror. And so the invention of the idea of revolution was in fact also, simultaneously, the invention of terror. There's an original link between the two that has been reproduced in various forms in everything that came afterward.

As for the Commune, the question is whether it was right or wrong when it hesitated the way it did about terror. That's a completely open question. The second point is that you have to see that the process Jean-Claude Milner described of the revolution's self-destruction, of its self-devouring – and the theme of the revolution devouring its own children is as old as revolution itself, as is the fact that revolutionary groups self-exterminate (just think of Condorcet, Danton, Robespierre, et al.) – is part and parcel of revolution. Why? Because the process of internal radicalization is immanent to it and, to some extent, necessarily uncontrolled. It's a fact that no revolution is able to regulate itself, because if it could, it wouldn't be a revolution. There would be none of those elements of upsurge, of unpredictability, of people mounting the stage of History who weren't on it before, and so on. It is well known that, during revolutions, the revolutionary leaders themselves are constantly on the alert and are only in control of a limited part of what is happening, hence the recourse to terror. All these phenomena are linked. Resorting to terror is always a measure of simplification and a way of attempting to do away with problems rather than to resolve them, no doubt about it. For all these reasons, I don't think the Cultural Revolution raises the issue of terror in any special or specific way. It's the whole of this history that involves the issue of terror.

What's nevertheless true is that the question of the Cultural Revolution's appropriation of the figure of revolution as such, including terror, in order to achieve communist goals (and not just proletarian or socialist ones) was bequeathed us by its very failure, in the same way as the Commune with its legacy of failure – which exposes it to criticism – bequeathed us the questions of organization, of the Party, of determining which organized form is capable of holding on to power and defeating the counter-revolutionary forces immediately arrayed against it. That's the situation we're in today.

Of course, when you've arrived at a position of political skepticism it's possible to think that the only question raised by the Cultural Revolution's failure is that of terror, now dealt with in terms of survival, of how bodies are treated, and so on. That's Jean-Claude Milner's perspective, which is what makes him concur with Simon Leys's point of view on that revolution. But from the standpoint of political thought, that assessment is superficial and irrelevant. The real question is that of the category of revolution and its contemporary relevance to the objectives of communist emancipation.

PP: *Alain Badiou, do you agree with Jean-Claude Milner when he underlines and affirms that the Cultural Revolution also paved the way for capitalism?*

AB: The failure of a revolution always paves the way for counter-revolution. Don't forget that during the Cultural Revolution Deng Xiaoping was regarded as "the top Party person in authority taking the capitalist road."[3] At the time, people made fun of such characterizations, but it was subsequently seen, when he took over power, that he was indeed, and even a lot more than could ever have been imagined, a top official taking the capitalist road. The label foisted on him by the Cultural Revolution was later proven to be completely accurate, and the defeat of the revolutionaries and the ultimate imprisonment of their leaders, the Gang of Four, ushered in a period of unbridled counter-revolution.

Now, what is a counter-revolution when the stakes are communist ones? It's capitalism! Because the chief contradiction is the one between capitalism and communism. I can't see any others. And, in fact, whether these phenomena were truly Chinese or not isn't a very important question, in my opinion. The goal of modernizing China, what Deng Xiaoping called "the "four modernizations," was really to make the country fit for the development of the most unbridled capitalism.

The Cultural Revolution was indeed responsible for that, in the sense that when any attempt – especially one of that size, duration, violence, and significance – fails, it creates favorable conditions for its opposite. That's inevitable. Likewise, the crushing of the Commune guided and stabilized the Third Republic in the republican, capitalistic, and imperialistic course it took.

---

[3] Deng was actually singled out by Mao as "the Number Two Party person in authority taking the capitalist road." The top honor went to Deng's mentor, Liu Shaoqui.

JCM: Is that only a nuance or not? I'd say it's more than that. Of course, I won't disagree with Alain Badiou about the fact that the defeat of a movement presenting itself as revolutionary leads to the victory of a movement that will present itself or be identified as counter-revolutionary. I'll skip the details; I consider this fact to be one of the basics of the physics of history, the physics of the forces that constitute historical processes. In this regard, I have no objection.

But I think there's an additional feature to the Cultural Revolution as I interpret it. It seems to me that the Cultural Revolution contained within it the elimination, as an analytical category, of the whole legacy – which can be considered good or bad – of what was called class analysis. In particular, I think the idea that the peasantry represented a cultural form that would hinder the establishment of a state-form, or in any case a revolutionary form of government, was latent in the Cultural Revolution. Of course, Deng Xiaoping developed his project in an extremely clear way, and he didn't bother with empty slogans. When he spoke about the "four modernizations" he took the bull by the horns. It reminds me of the clarity with which Napoleon Bonaparte, at the time of the Consulate, wrote: "The Revolution is over." Basically, that was pretty much exactly what Deng Xiaoping wanted to get across. But above and beyond the mere phenomenon of reaction associated with failure, there was something more: the conviction that the Chinese peasantry had to disappear. Deng Xiaoping stated that conviction, but it had already taken root in the Cultural Revolution.

AB: That's a total exaggeration as far as the Cultural Revolution is concerned. Let me mention two phenomena in this connection.

First of all, there's the fact that the countryside remained, to all intents and purposes, on the sidelines of the Cultural Revolution. And it remained on the

sidelines in accordance with the express wishes of the
Maoist leaders. The Cultural Revolution was first a
student and academic phenomenon, arising from what
can be called the youth movement, and later a workers'
movement. Factories and universities were the key sites
of the revolution, as they were, moreover, in May '68
in France. The few scattered attempts to define something like the Cultural Revolution in the countryside
failed and played no part in the whole affair, to the
point where, when it became clear that factional
struggle – the most anarchic and bloody mode of the
Cultural Revolution, involving student factions above
all – was leading to chaos, these factions were sent to
the country. We're talking about an enormous operation: almost all the Red Guards were sent to the country.
And the ideological motivation driving that decision
was exactly the opposite of what you said it was. The
source of the factor of stabilization, of reconstruction
of a tenable and acceptable order, was the countryside,
as Mao Zedong had always thought, introducing new
ideas in this regard. Let's not forget, on this score,
Mao Zedong's extremely harsh criticisms of Stalin, virtually all of which concerned the fact that Stalin
despised the peasants and had subjected them to such
constraints that he'd destabilized and terrorized society
as a whole. I think that the peasant dimension of original Maoism was maintained during the period of the
Cultural Revolution despite the extremist efforts of
some Red Guard groups. Those Red Guards were
moreover subjected to extremely violent state repression toward the end.

PP: *Allow me to quote one of your formulations, Alain
Badiou: "The understanding of massacres, and therefore the possibility that they won't recur, forces us to
come back to the understanding of politics properly
speaking, that is – let's face it – to what the ideas of the
Nazis were." You were speaking about Nazism then.*

The history of massacres does not end, unfortunately, with Nazism, or with the Gulag or Rwanda. Given this ineluctable killing frenzy, do you now acknowledge the progress of the legal and philosophical conscience? In your opinion, is the emergence of the category of "crime against humanity" part of this understanding of the political that you were calling for?

AB: No, I don't think so at all. I think that the juridification – like the moralization, moreover – of phenomena of political violence has never contributed in any crucial way to our understanding them. The categories dealing with massacres, which are roughly the categories having to do with the theory of human rights, are currently tacked on to situations in such a way that these situations remain unintelligible. In the final analysis, it's only about legitimizing outside military intervention then. No understanding is introduced by the simple observation that, in this or that region of the world, the survival of the population, of the speaking bodies, as Jean-Claude Milner would put it, is not assured, especially when such an observation is based on a handful of TV images, however horrific they may be. We have no idea why things are happening that way, nor what the opposing forces at work locally are, nor whether it's a civil war or a foreign incursion, nor what the underlying stakes are in terms, for example, of particular raw materials or energy sources, nor who's supplying the arms.

As regards the relationship between states and the causes of conventional warfare, there may be some demonstrable merit in the efforts to establish international law, efforts which, incidentally, go way back, but that doesn't represent any progress in terms of political intelligibility. I even think it adds to the confusion, because the question that's left hanging is who the executive agents of the law are. The fact is, it's the great powers and they alone.

PP: *There was nevertheless a Nuremberg moment, the progressive recognition of the right to rights, the possibility of criticizing the law of the state. Can't that recognition be connected with some political or philosophical reason?*

AB: Let me repeat: the right to rights is for the time being the right of the great powers and the right of the victors. That's absolutely clear. The so-called "international community" today, this imperious new subject that lays down the law on a global scale, is a coalition of powers – so much so that the "real" great powers are explicitly exempt from this so-called law. Has anyone from France, the UK, or America ever been prosecuted? Or anyone from China nowadays? Yet those countries have committed – and very recently, too – a great many crimes: thousands of civilians have died from their bombs and in their prisons; they've openly plotted political assassinations; they've bankrolled torturers . . . Everyone knows as much. But everyone also knows that you won't be tried unless you're a citizen of a small country, or a defeated country.

The coalition of powers is a well-known secret government, which is moreover part of the restoration, today, of a nineteenth-century-type context in which, now that the basic antagonism between the socialist and imperialist camps has disappeared, it's in actual fact a matter of maneuvering and of negotiating a balance among the great powers in a new international arena completely dominated by capital, the market, and the cynicism of power. To speak of "law" in such a context is totally bogus.

PP: *Would you say the same about the 1948 Universal Declaration of Human Rights? Didn't it create a specific historical opening?*

AB: No, I don't think so. I think that to understand our current situation, as far as international matters are concerned, you have to go a lot further back, to the consequences of the Treaty of Versailles after World War I, to the creation of the Society of Nations and what ensued. And I think that a new doctrine of world peace emerged at that time, a doctrine that succeeded the purely European notion of a balance of powers while preserving its main principle: power lays down the law.

The so-called Western powers are regarded as the general legal bastion laying down the law everywhere else in the world, but, as they're also the ones who are at the root of power, the coalition between power and law is inherently suspect. Besides, when dealing with anyone or anything that's just as powerful or too powerful, the law suspends its effects as suddenly as it was invoked.

PP: *Let me put the question a different way. Do you absolutely reject the right to rights? Or the struggle of a man like Paul Bouchet, who was a resistance fighter in the Forez region, the FLN's defense attorney during the Algerian War, and someone I'd venture to call a "French voice of conscience," someone who was not a "human rightist" as that term is generally understood but instead believed and thought that the right to rights could advance the consciousness of peoples . . .*

AB: I fully agree with that perspective and am in favor of support for and the implementation of a concept of the right to rights. The question, the one I'm asking, is who the operative subject is in all this business. If there were a Communist International with recognized symbolic sovereignty, I'd be a very strong proponent of the right to rights. But while the only executive body remains a coalition of powers, I'm suspicious of it. And I have testimonies and abundant proof to back up the legitimacy of that suspicion. For the time being, the predominant activity of coalitions of this sort has consisted in destroying and carving up states – such as Yugoslavia, Iraq, Afghanistan, Somalia, Libya, and so on.

PP: *Even the International Criminal Tribunal (ICT)?*[4]

AB: Yes, even the Tribunal, which only tries minor personalities who have been defeated, which is the reason why I urge that it be dissolved, just as I urge that NATO, moreover, and even the UN in its present form, be dissolved.

PP: *Jean-Claude Milner, what do you think about this issue?*

JCM: I'm going to go back to that statement of Alain Badiou's that you reminded us of, namely, the idea that the understanding of massacres might help prevent their recurrence. That's a point I don't agree with at all. I think that the understanding of massacres is something fundamental, but it has no preventive or therapeutic benefit of any kind, precisely because I'm basically in agreement with what I think Alain Badiou's thesis is, namely that if there are massacres, it's because there are powers, and that it doesn't come from some inner propensity of human beings driving them to kill or from some unfortunate conjunction of circumstances.

That said, I'd like to point out, in connection with the so-called Nuremberg moment, that it's an interesting and important moment as regards the very conception of law: it marks the end of Roman law.

In Roman law, the source of the law was state power, whereas in the Nuremberg trials, the Germanic, or at any rate Anglo-Saxon, conception prevailed, i.e., the law has its own source, independent of state power. In Roman law, the law could take precedence over state

---

[4]Philippe Petit refers here to the Tribunal pénal international. Three such tribunals have been established specifically for trying individuals for genocide, crimes against humanity, and war crimes in the former Yugoslavia, Rwanda, and Sierra Leone, respectively. The International Criminal Court (ICC) is the permanent tribunal.

power if the state consented to limit itself; in Anglo-Saxon law the consent or non-consent of the state isn't required. One of the participants in the Nuremberg trials fully understood that they were switching from one conception of law to another, that it was an "American-style" trial that was involved, and that the notion of "pleading guilty" was essential if you wanted to save your skin. I'm thinking of Albert Speer. He pleaded guilty, which enabled him to cover up a good deal of what he'd really done, in order to save his skin and ultimately to publish a bestseller. He even became a leading figure in the international moral order. But the driving force behind "pleading guilty" is bargaining. Speer literally bargained for his life. In fact, his public repentance was not just useful for him; it validated the process as a whole. The Nuremberg trials were legitimized by what Speer revealed, but the truthfulness of what he revealed was guaranteed by his repentance.

International tribunals in general function on the model of the Nuremberg trials. They are based on a conception of law that consists in not examining the way in which the tribunal is constituted, since you only have to say that it's the law in order not to have to be concerned about where it comes from and for it to take precedence over states. A positivist would wonder where this power of the law comes from. That's what Churchill's objection was: he was against the Nuremberg trials, saying they were all about the justice of the victors. In that respect, he remained a traditional European. At all events, the trials took place and they remain the horizon in which we're inscribed.

AB: I completely agree with Jean-Claude Milner about that, but I'd just add one minor reservation: you have to understand that all this means that the law comes into the picture here not in terms of its connection with politics, with political intelligibility, but in terms of its connection with subjective morality. As a result, bargaining about what one did and repentance have to be crucial components of the subjectivity of the person who's on trial if he wants to save his skin. I completely agree that this Nuremberg moment marked a break in the figure of law. But, as is always the case with the American tradition, what occurred at that moment was, so to speak, generically biblical. And in any case, by the way, I think the US is a country that has no idea whatsoever what politics is, but that's another story . . .

JCM: That's another issue we wouldn't disagree about, so it's not all that interesting . . . Likewise, I agree about thinking in terms of specific cases: the fact that there are humanitarian corridors, that there are foreign interventions – it all has to be judged on a case-by-case basis. We'd surely disagree about how we evaluated the different cases: where one of us would say yes, the other would say no, but that's another issue.

To go back to international justice, I maintain that "pleading guilty" is its cornerstone. Someone like Albert Speer who is smart enough to admit that what he did was evil will benefit from the well-known principle that when you're in a position of weakness you're better off admitting half of what you did. That way you'll avoid having the other half scrutinized. But the fact is, thus far I haven't seen many accused heads of state who have gone about things that way before a tribunal. They've generally chosen to stick to their position, which has resulted in their death or imprisonment. In that respect, international justice rarely achieves its goal and is often disappointing. This, as a result, leads to the use of bricolage. Since international opinion expects some variant of the "pleading guilty" principle in the guise of repentance, and since pleading guilty is all about bargaining, bargaining is the horizon of international justice. The person who's in a position of weakness has to accept losing something in order to save something. That's usually the offer he's made, and, as experience has shown that repentance before a tribunal is rare, they try to spare him the tribunal. That's what they did with Tunisian president Ben Ali: if you agree to leave, you can keep your wife and your lavish lifestyle. And the same thing is looming, even as we speak, for Syria's president, Bashir al-Assad.

PP: *But is bricolage the same thing as a contract?*

JCM: If we get away from the daily aspect of newspapers and look at principles instead, the noble word for bargaining is in fact "contract." Bargaining is actually a contract. So why did the Nuremberg moment take such a form? It's also because the reigning idea was that political forms are contractual. And when I say contractual, I don't mean in the sense of Rousseau's social contract; I mean an Anglo-Saxon-type contract, a deal – and I say that without any contempt. The contract rather than the law. It's moreover clear that, ultimately, the Nuremberg trials applied no prior law. They took place within the framework of a contract accepted by the victors – and eventually by the losers as well. The Nazi regime wasn't alone among the ideological and intellectual losers of the Nuremberg trials: the whole European doctrine of the state was sidelined.

PP: *Let's change perspectives, if it's all right with you. Alain Badiou, in your preface to the new edition of* Le Concept de modèle[5] *you make a connection between the waning of your revolutionary fervor in the early 1970s and your rediscovery of mathematics, to which you ascribe a reparative and calming function. And in your lecture devoted to the enigmatic relationship between philosophy and politics, you claim that mathematics is probably the best paradigm of justice there is. In this*

---

[5] Alain Badiou, "Préface de la nouvelle édition," *Le Concept de modèle* (Paris: Fayard, 2007).

regard, you note that "a proof is a proof, for anyone whatsoever, without exception, who accepts the primitive choice and the logical rules. Thus, we obtain the notions of choice, consequences, equality, and universality."[6] *That, in your opinion, is the paradigm of classical revolutionary politics, the aim of which is justice. The basic choice must be accepted. Is what's valid for classical politics equally valid for contemporary politics, in your opinion?*

AB: That's the key problem, which is not entirely unrelated to what we were discussing a moment ago. I think we're going through a crisis of traditional politics. And this crisis encompasses the modern form of traditional politics in its representative, parliamentary, multiparty, and so on, guise, but also all the different forms of representation of revolutionary politics, which, in its classical phase, nonetheless shared a basic principle of representation with its adversaries. The basic principle was that social forces were politically concentrated in organized forms whose ultimate aim was to become masters of the state apparatus. Oddly enough, this view of things was shared by practically everyone at a certain moment in the twentieth century. If the Cold War was cold, it was in the final analysis because something about the conception of the state was shared by both sides. And that allowed for a war of negotiation, which is to say a war in which, at any given moment, the weakness of one side could negotiate with the weakness of the other.

That set-up gradually entered a crisis. And in fact I think that some aspects of the contemporary uprisings – May '68, the Cultural Revolution, and even the uprisings in the Arab countries – are distinct, specific episodes of that crisis. It was a crisis of the relationship

[6] Alain Badiou, *Philosophy for Militants*, trans. Bruno Bosteels (London and New York: Verso, 2012), 33.

between politics and the state since, at bottom, in the traditional conception, state power is at stake in the potentially antagonistic conflict between the political forces embodied in their respective organized forms, which go by the generic name "party." That's why the key concept, from the standpoint of the popular, proletarian – call it whatever you like – side is revolution, inasmuch as revolution designates the moment when the possibility opened up that this goal, the state, might be attainable, that is, might be able to be captured, seized, destroyed, and reorganized.

I think that, for the reasons I already mentioned, the Cultural Revolution marked the end of that state of affairs, because, once a certain threshold of the political issues at stake had been reached, the process in question was no longer valid. While it's true that the communist hypothesis, in all its forms, is linked to a process of withering away of the state, it's hard to see how it could be achieved by the sole means of seizing state power. Ironically, it could be argued that one of the sources of terror is the paradoxical position of the appropriation of state power by a force whose doctrine is based on the idea of the dissolution, or the renunciation, of that same power. This is something that's always experienced as danger, as a threat, as enemy infiltration or the Japanese spy, and so on.

So all that sort of thing has to be done away with, which means, for the period that's beginning – and I have no idea what its outcome will be – that politics must remain at a strict distance from the state. It cannot accept for its immediate goal to be the seizure of power, and it must shun all procedures that, as such, propose that hypothesis or option to it. Let's say that the end of traditional politics involves the establishment of a new adjustment, a new distance, a unique strategy of separation between what could be called the political process properly speaking – which is always an inter-popular process linked to movements, watchwords, and organizations – and the state, which, in my opinion, it's far more important to restrain than to seize. And in that sense, we're no longer dealing with a three-term logic, namely, popular action, organizations, and state power.

We'll gradually move toward a two-term logic involving the state figure – its system of power and maneuvering – and the political process as distance, as organized exteriority. As a result, the phase that's beginning must be regarded as an in-between phase since it's absolutely experimental: even the doctrinal components characterizing the new situation are still pretty meager. This is the assessment that can be made not just of recent incidents in political life but also of the historical sequence we were talking about before: roughly speaking, the one that began with the French Revolution.

PP: *Consequently, the ideal of justice is reconfigured . . .*

AB: The ideal of justice is utterly reconfigured insofar as its paradigm is no longer the figure of the "good state." Already in Plato, and to an even greater extent in Aristotle, the figure of justice was closely correlated with the figure of the "good state." That paradigm was still the socialist states' paradigm, it must be said. That's why the last Chinese revolution called itself, oddly enough, a "cultural" revolution: it was a matter of a subjective and ideological revolution, not just of transitioning from a bad state to a better one. That radical novelty bequeathed a problem to us that's extremely difficult to solve, namely, what is the definition of justice when it can no longer be embodied in the figure of the good state, the benevolent state?

PP: *Jean-Claude Milner, do you agree with this idea of an in-between phase?*

JCM: On a descriptive level it's possible, but I'm not sure I'd pose the questions that way, even if I might agree on a number of points. I think that, as regards political representations, the primacy of the notion of state has never been entirely right. It's right for what I'd call European, or Continental, political thought; that is, the sphere that was affected in a lasting way by the French Revolution and its aftermath – which means that Great Britain isn't really part of it. But these are just minor reservations. The second point, and this one should no doubt be stressed, is that, to the extent that the communist hypothesis is meaningless for me, it's obvious that everything about this issue that depends on the relationship between the validity of that hypothesis and the validity or non-validity of the state – all considerations of that sort don't matter for me. One final aspect of my distance from it is the issue of justice and the way the mathematical paradigm takes over from the state paradigm in Badiou's system of thought. But, if I may say so, I'm not about to play second fiddle to Badiou's approach!

PP: *In what sense is turning to mathematics useful? For you, Alain Badiou, the subject is closely related to formal operations whose resources mathematics alone can allow us to glimpse. What separates the two of you or brings you together with respect to this issue of turning to mathematics and of its effects on the subject?*

AB: When I spoke biographically about mathematics as a means of relief and calming for me with respect to the disorders and failures of politics, it didn't mean that there is any relationship whatsoever between mathematics and politics. The opposite is even the case. What I meant was that, by turning my thought toward something that was utterly different from politics, mathematics could temporarily act as a kind of personal therapy.

Let me remind you that, for me, mathematics, the science of the pure multiple, the science of the formula of multiplicity as such, is ontology. What's at issue in

mathematics is being *qua* being, and that's something
that's only remotely involved in apparatuses of thought
like art or politics, which operate within determinate
worlds – even if, of course, mathematics is one of the
conditions of philosophy, and one of the most important, as can be seen from Plato to Husserl or me. But
it's only with very specific speculative mediations that
you can establish a link, as Plato does, between mathematics and politics in philosophy, without mathematics
ever achieving the position of a direct condition for
politics itself.

JCM: I'm not sure that anything more than a distance
can be marked between us here, since, for me, mathematics, which I in no way claim to pursue on as deep a
level as Badiou does, has no importance other than for
mathematics itself. I don't think it provides any insight
outside of mathematics itself. So, where this is concerned, I can only mark a distance between us . . .

AB: A very anti-philosophical distance moreover,
because it actually amounts to dismissing out of hand
a deeply rooted conviction, at least from Plato to myself,
that mathematics is, on the contrary, extremely important in the history of thinking humanity's development.
So much so that people as different from each other as
Spinoza, Kant, and Husserl have said that if mathematics hadn't existed, philosophy would have been impossible. This anti-philosophical idea of yours is even odder
in that you haven't always had it, Jean-Claude, or so it
seems to me. What's more, it's lacking any proof whatsoever, and it's even obviously false. It's clear that mathematics is everywhere in our immediate environment
today. The simplest technical object is the result of an
extremely sophisticated mathematical configuration; the
most basic telephone presupposes a great number of
calculations. The material world itself was radically
changed by what you have called the "power of the

letter." To do without mathematics is to accept being totally ignorant about the basic functioning of the world around us.

JCM: They're two different questions, in my opinion. I agree, that wasn't always my position. I remember very well an earlier debate we had a really long time ago, which you "won." It was in the early 1990s, right after the fall of the Berlin Wall. I had just published *Constat*. Our match had been pretty even up until the moment when you pointed out that in *Constat* I had used the notion of the infinite and you objected that I wasn't taking account of what mathematics teaches us about it. I replied that I hadn't meant the infinite in the mathematical sense of the term. My saying that was regarded as a defeat – and rightly so, because my answer was negative. What I should have said, and what I'd say now, is that the notion of the infinite is only of interest to the extent that mathematics doesn't take it over.

AB: Which has always been, let me just note in passing, theology's point of view.

JCM: I don't deny it. Back then, I'm embarrassed to admit, I hadn't read Jonas Cohen's book *Histoire de l'infini*, which I've since read. It dates from the end of the nineteenth century and presents itself as a history of the infinite in Western thought up to Kant. In fact, it stops with Georg Cantor because, it's implied, the history of the infinite comes to an end once a clear and distinct mathematical concept becomes established.

It's absolutely true that for a long time I accepted that something could be learned from mathematics. I'm not talking about application, measurement, mathematization, and so forth. I'm referring to the possibility that new philosophical propositions might be obtained on the basis of wholly mathematical procedures and concepts. This conviction came from the *Cahiers pour l'analyse*. Like Jacques-Alain Miller, Badiou, and Lacan himself, but with a very weak background in mathematics compared with them, I thought that what was happening in mathematics in general and in the philosophy of mathematics in particular was not only extremely interesting (which I still believe) but essential. I hadn't yet concluded that the logic of my position required me to say that mathematics is essential for mathematics itself, and for it alone.

The material importance you're talking about is connected with the mathematization of physics, whose centrality for physics I'm not unaware of – far from it. After all, I often refer to Koyré. But the mathematization of physics is precisely *not* the whole of mathematics. Regardless of whether or not a mathematical, or rather mathematized, physics existed, mathematics could still go on.

PP: *But could you both give your opinions as to the question of the infinite?*

AB: I think Jean-Claude expressed his position clearly when he said that the concept of the infinite, as such, is only of interest to the extent that mathematics hasn't appropriated it. What he has in mind is a genealogy, a history, in which mathematics doesn't play an essential role, whereas I think exactly the opposite is true.

I think the concept of the infinite was vague and linked to theological discursivity up until the time when it started to be progressively mathematized, and at that point it entered the system of rational thinking from which it had been excluded. It's only natural that, in a mathematics that wasn't really concerned yet with the question of the infinite, the Greeks recognized the validity of a finitistic hypothesis about the organization of the cosmos. There's a sort of latent axiom of finitude in Greek thought, linked to the fact that mathematics could not yet make the concept of infinity rational. The rational history of the infinite began in a distinct way in the seventeenth century. It was through differential and integral calculus that the question of infinity was reintroduced not only into mathematics but into the mathematization of physics, almost simultaneously, moreover, with Leibniz and Newton.

From then on, the history of the infinite became inseparable from the already extensive history of a rational concept. I would note that this history is by no means over, since for the past 30 years, thanks to astonishing theorems that have been proved by a plethora of mathematicians of genius (Solovay, Martin, Jensen, Kunen, Woodin, et al.), there have still been major transformations of this concept at the most fundamental level, that of the hierarchy of types of infinity. There's really a disagreement between us on this subject, but I'll refrain from going into detail about it till later because of Jean-Claude Milner's reintroduction of a certain amount of theology into his own conceptual apparatus. As a matter of fact, I think there are only two options when it comes to this question of the infinite: the mathematical perspective or the theological perspective. I don't think there's a third position that can be maintained. And I also interpret along similar lines things that we'll perhaps discuss some other time, like the statement that contemporary historicity is entirely bound up with the return of the name "Jew," i.e., a figure that continues to hang on, so to speak, to divine election, to an elective conception of both the infinite and universality.

PP: *Jean-Claude Milner, what you now think about the universal is the culmination of a long process. Could you recall some of its twists and turns for us?*

JCM: Let's make a distinction, so that the debate will be clear, between the question of the infinite and that of the universal – even if the (definite) disagreements pitting us against each other on the question of the infinite are eventually intertwined with our (potential) disagreement on the question of the universal.

As far as the universal is concerned, it did in fact have to do with a process for me, a subjective process. One day I asked myself about it, because, as I was reading the texts, I had the feeling that the reference to the universal in Kant, for example, functioned by itself as an operator of clarity. To bring the relevance of the universal to light, to pose a question from the standpoint of the universal, to universalize the argument: that was the first step in an enterprise of clarifying and distinguishing. For me, the first step consisted in calling that first step into question and asking myself: "Is the universal itself clear and distinct?" From that point on, I sought to determine the conditions of clarity and distinction that would make it possible to answer: "Yes, the universal is a clear and distinct notion." Over the course of the process I was led to combine this inquiry with another, completely separate, more anecdotal one, which involved all the uncertainties that were stirred up in me by Lacan's writings about the all [*le tout*], and in particular the hypothesis that there is not one way to write the all but two.

In a sense, I combined these two lines of questioning. I don't mean that I reflected on the universal in order to explain Lacan or that I reflected on Lacan in order to clear up my confusion about the universal. I simply assumed, spurred on by Lacan, that the concept of the universal wouldn't be clear and distinct unless it was recognized that there are several different concepts of the universal and that each lays down specific conditions for its own intelligibility. Once I had thought that, I immersed myself in certain texts again, and that led me to realize that I had basic points of disagreement with Alain Badiou about the use of the concept of the universal.

3

The Infinite, the Universal, and the Name "Jew"

PP: *To get the ball rolling again, I'd like to clarify with you, Jean-Claude Milner, your relationship to mathematics in general and to the notion of the infinite in particular. As I was reading* Constat *(1992) again, I was struck by the fact that the book concludes with the project of scrutinizing the ethics of the maximum, whose distinguishing feature is that it's an ethics incorporated within the question of politics. Your intention, however, was to separate the two. You added another imperative to the project: "It must also be separated from the question of the infinite for the subject," you wrote. Could you clarify this point and explain how you differ from Alain Badiou on this?*

JCM: That book gave rise to a debate between Alain Badiou and me at the Collège de philosophie. On that occasion, I realized that I hadn't grasped all the implications of my own position. *Constat* is based on the notion of the infinite as it operates in the Galilean Revolution. I borrowed from Koyré the notion of an infinite universe, which he developed in *From the Closed World to the Infinite Universe* (1957; English translation 1968).

I pointed out that the French Revolution was tied, explicitly in the works of its foremost representatives, to the possibility of modern science, which is to say, at that time, to the possibility of a mathematized physics. As the French Revolution defined the scope of politics in the nineteenth and most of the twentieth century, as it placed the notion of revolution itself in the position of a fundamental political criterion, it simultaneously accorded political significance to the infinite: it made it the basis of maximality in political will and thought.

I stand by all this today, but I'd add a rectification. At that time, I hadn't thematized a sort of time lag, a dyschronia, clearly enough. When mathematized physics started to reflect on the infinite universe, mathematicians had only a vague, fuzzy notion of infinity. Leibniz spoke about "the labyrinth of infinity"; Newton had to use God to get out of the predicament; Kant's thinking was based on the possibility of Newtonian physics, and when he linked the questions of infinity and freedom closely together, it was clear to him that he had nothing to learn about infinity from the mathematicians. Sure, they made use of infinity in infinitesimal calculus, but they didn't know what it was all about. There was a disparity between the fact that infinity functioned very productively in calculus and the fact that there was no mathematical theory of infinity. It might be assumed that Kantian philosophy sought to account for this disparity, but that need not concern us here.

There was an awareness of this overall situation in *Constat*, but it wasn't asserted as such. I am asserting it now. It's precisely to the extent that infinity wasn't a clear and distinct mathematical concept that it was able to serve as a reference point in both classical philosophy and mathematized physics. It's paradoxical that physics became mathematized and, in so doing, opened the possibility for an infinite universe, and yet it didn't know, in mathematical terms, what the infinite was. This was the point on which Alain Badiou stuck it to me in 1992 – and rightly so, since it was a weak link in my framework back then.

I've now changed it, in my own opinion, into a strong link, by claiming that maximality and infinity can only overlap if the infinite doesn't have a clear status in mathematics. As soon as it enjoys a clear status in mathematics, either you choose to be indifferent to mathematics or you disregard the infinite. This can lead to thinking about the infinite in non-mathematical terms. That's what I've done, and I'm not the only one who has. In Badiou's case, on the contrary, the argument seems to me to be as follows: (1) in both philosophy and politics, a clear and distinct idea of the infinite is necessary; (2) only mathematics provides a clear and distinct idea of the infinite; (3) mathematics is central for both philosophy and politics.

AB: The question of the infinite is in fact an absolutely central issue for me, and I intend to elaborate further on it in my future work. It's central because of its direct connection with the category of truth. In my framework, any truth is a set of a generic (hence universal) nature, and the infiniteness of such a set is an intrinsic requirement. Any truth procedure, as a result, is uncompletable. This is, moreover, why truths travel through time and space – not just because their universality is recognized, but because they are pursued and further developed and their implications examined in a variety of ways.

Ultimately, it is crucial to separate the infinite from the One, to have done with theology, to think the multiplicity of infinities. Indeed, we know that there are infinities of different types whose relationship, combination, and complexity are involved in any genuine truth. It's absolutely essential for philosophy to grasp the mathematical clarification of the concept of infinity, a progressive clarification that began with Cantor and the investigation of which is not yet complete, since over the course of the past 20 years significant progress and changes have occurred in contemporary mathematics where this issue is concerned.

PP: *But why, once "the endless counting to infinity," ["l'infini de promenade"]¹ as you, Alain Badiou, call it, has been eliminated, does this thinking of infinity necessarily encounter the theory of the subject?*

AB: Once you define a subject as what an individual, a human animal, becomes when they are incorporated into a truth procedure (this is the terminology of *Logics of Worlds*) or when you define the subject, in the terminology of *Being and Event*, as a local point of a truth procedure, you understand that a subject is always confronted with the infinite, for the reason I mentioned before, namely, the uncompletable, and therefore infinite, nature of every truth.

PP: *Why do you reject that assumption, Jean-Claude Milner?*

JCM: In my framework, the notions of maximum and minimum determine the most important issue, the primary issue. The infinite is one of the versions of the maximum; it's the one that has been prevalent ever since the time when the hypothesis that the universe was infinite became bound up with the possibility of modern science. From Rousseau, say, and the French Revolution on, politics was torn between two competing appeals: either it could look to the ancient world or it could look to the modern universe. The French Revolution, as far as both its discourses and actions were concerned, really oscillated constantly between these two appeals.

On one side, you have the reference to the Greek city and the Roman republic, and, on the other, you have

¹ See Alain Badiou, *Le Fini et l'infini* (Paris: Bayard, 2010).

the clear perception of a kind of modernity. There were two features about this modernity that the Enlightenment thinkers had connected and that the Revolution disconnected, without, however, giving up either of them: science (mathematized physics), on the one hand, and the commodity form, on the other – Newton and Adam Smith, if you will. As I often point out, the nationalization of the clergy's property amounted to dumping an enormous quantity of land holdings into the sphere of commodities, since these were to be sold in order to replenish public finances. The ancient-world appeal, as can easily be seen, would instead have led to making the clergy's property a commodity-free zone. So there was this oscillation. I could further show that the discovery of the commodity form was inscribed in the promotion of infinity that mathematized physics had undertaken.

So-called political economy is based on the axiom that the Newtonian infinite universe and the global market are one and the same thing. The question is whether or not Marx, and Lenin after him, accepted this axiom. I think they did, even though I note in passing that, in my view, it is utterly false, but now's not the time to discuss that. If you want to describe the paradigm of revolution in general, that axiom must be taken into account. There is a consequence that follows from all this, namely that, given that revolution must push political subjects to the maximum of their will and knowledge, modern revolution will be steeped in the assumption, "The maximum is the infinite." But I think that, today, the minimum/maximum opposition can and must be separated from the question of the infinite.

In my approach, the notions of "more than" and "less than" are critical. But they're not mathematical notions. If the notion of "surplus value" [*plus-value*] is to mean anything, the "more" [*plus*] involved cannot be mathematical. I'm not sure, incidentally, whether it is for Marx himself, but in any case it's not mathematizable. The opposition "more than"/"less than" – and therefore maximum/minimum – is more important for me than the question of the infinite. Hence, my final comment: the question of the maximum must be separated from that of the infinite because the question of the infinite is merely one of the historically documented forms of the maximum.

PP: *A separation like that will nevertheless lead to "the politics of things," and although the point of departure is clearly the same for both of you, the end point isn't.*

JCM: Our point of departure isn't the same, since the maximum/minimum opposition is completely irrelevant as far as Alain Badiou is concerned.

AB: I take issue with that remark. The opposition between maximum and minimum is completely relevant for me, not, of course, on the level of pure multiplicity, which is the level of ontology, but as regards worldly particularity, the intensity with which a given multiple-object appears in a determinate world. In *Logics of Worlds* I established that the transcendental evaluation of anything in a determinate world occurs within a framework that consists of a maximum and a minimum. It is on the basis of the maximum that something can be said to belong absolutely to a world and on the basis of the minimum that this thing, although being in the world, can nevertheless be said to be regarded as inexistent in it, since its degree of belonging to that world is minimal.

My difference from Milner therefore has to do with the *organization* of the levels rather than with their nature per se. To sum up: the infinite is an ontological predicate of the being-multiple considered in itself, whereas the maximum and the minimum are among the main operators of the worldly analytic. What we're dealing with here is precisely the issue of universality and particularity, or of universality and singularity. Let's say – this is unavoidable – that a truth procedure constructs universality out of particular materials and that the becoming of a universal truth occurs in immanence to particular situations. This is a simple consequence of the fact that a truth, of any kind, appears in a particular world. This dialectic is intelligible only if the procedure is stratified. There's an ontological level on which the infinite is normative, and there's a level I call "appearing," which is simply the worldliness of the thing, its particularity, in which the maximum and the minimum are fundamental operators.

JCM: But you can easily see the point on which we differ cropping up here, it seems to me: it's the fact that I don't have an affirmative ontology.

PP: *But doesn't that operation lead you to a gradual distancing from the philosophical gesture, Jean-Claude Milner?*

JCM: It can be presented that way, but that's not the driving force behind it. When I say I don't have an affirmative ontology that doesn't mean I don't put forward ontological-type propositions. Hence the importance I can attach to something seemingly insignificant but which might have major consequences. I'm referring to the Saussurian position.

Perhaps without realizing the implications of what he was saying, Saussure defined a type of being that is related only to difference. This gave rise to what I call a *mis-ontology*, on the basis of either the Greek negation *me* or the French negation *mé-* that's found in words like *méforme* [unfitness], *méconnaissance* [misrecognition], and so on. Such an ontology completely rejects the assumption that being and the One are linked to each other. By the same token, it strips the question of their mutual genealogy of its central importance: "Do we begin with the One and then continue with being, or vice-versa?" and so on. If I have an ontology, it's not an affirmative one in the sense that Alain Badiou's might be. It doesn't define a level. It's separate from what Alain Badiou calls the "worldly level."

AB: Note that, on this specific issue of ontology, we're in uneasy proximity to each other rather than in radical opposition. Why? Because the operation of separating being from the One is constitutive of my own project just as it is of Milner's. This is possibly the only point – an essentially a-theological one – on which we agree. To the extent that in our thinking there are a few remnants of ontology, dispersive where Jean-Claude Milner is concerned or systematic where I'm concerned, these remnants will in any case have to be compatible with the separation of being and the One, essentially in a differential way for Jean-Claude Milner and essentially in a multifaceted appearing for me. This point should be stressed since it's precisely from within this local agreement between us that our subsequent huge disagreement takes on its meaning.

PP: *That disagreement comes up again in connection with the notion of "universal," which, may I remind you, wasn't yet a "key word" for you, Jean-Claude Milner, when* Les Noms indistincts (1983) *came out. But it would become one later on.*

JCM: Yes. You're right to point out that it hadn't yet appeared in *Les Noms indistincts*. I only gradually confronted what seemed to me to be concealed in most approaches. It is generally accepted that the notion of the infinite merits reflection; the notion of the universal, on the other hand, seems to be regarded as clear and distinct in itself. To show how this is by no means the case, let me take a simple example. When the Universal Declaration of the Rights of Man was published, it was assumed that "universal" was clear in and of itself. Yet many different things can be meant by "universal." It can mean that the declaration applies by extension to all human beings, now and to come – in other words, that human beings *qua* the many can and must adhere to the declaration: you begin with the universal understood extensionally and then say that there are universal rights. But it can also be understood intensionally: the declaration defines the notion of human being. What's more, it defines it as human beings' capacity for the universal. In this sense, you don't begin with rights and say that they're universal; you begin with the universal and say that there are rights. The upshot is that you don't know what it is you're talking about. This isn't a criticism, it's just an observation. I'm even prepared to accept that it would be better for an institution not to set itself an ideal of clarity and distinction. However, intellectual reflection imposes different criteria on itself.

I was led to the conclusion that the notion of the universal demands as much attention as the notion of the infinite. In mathematics, the latter notion began to become clear as soon as several different types of infinity were introduced. That was Cantor's feat, owing to which infinity is no longer expressed in the singular but in the plural. Similarly, I tried to argue that the universal could be expressed in several possible ways, and that these weren't all equivalent. That led me to focus criticism on positions that seemed to me to ignore this. I'll let Alain Badiou correct me if need be, but in my interpretation of his thinking, I had the impression that the universal was homogeneous with itself, while the infinite wasn't.

AB: Oh, come on! The idea that the notion of the universal needs to be revised, transformed, and examined was *my* idea originally! In particular, I don't feel Jean-Claude Milner's reflections on the analytic type of universality apply in any way to me. I absolutely don't think that universality is the universal quantification of judgments. Universality isn't the "for all x" of a supposedly universal judgment. For me, universality, that is, the possible predicate of a truth, is always a construction, a procedure, which unfolds in a particular situation or world. Universality is always built with materials that are particular. What's more, this construction immediately comes up against the infinite – that effective dialectic of universality and the infinite – because of the fact that it's uncompletable.

There are thus three basic attributes of universality. First, only a procedure connected with a particular world, a particular construction, can be called universal. Second, this particular construction, insofar as it is uncompletable, is of the register of infinity, whatever the type of infinity concerned. And third, *qua* universal, a particular truth is not wholly reducible to the particularity of the world in which it is created. Clearly, it's this last bit that has interested philosophy ever since Plato: what is a construction that occurs in a particular world and that is nevertheless not reducible to the parameters of that particular world? This is the question Marx asked in the introduction to the *Grundrisse*: why does Greek art affect us even though it speaks to us, in a dead language, of a world we no longer know, a world that has become altogether impenetrable for us? Or: why is Euclidean mathematics perfectly intelligible to us? How is it that the anthropological context of these artistic or scientific productions in no way exhausts their ability to be communicated and transmitted? So it could be said that the universality of a truth is that which constitutes an exception to the anthropological hold of a particularity, or to the hold of a historical and cultural world, to the hold of the context in which it is constructed.

The key to the whole thing is, first, a theory of the immanent exception: what has the ability to be an exception to a given anthropological context? My answer is: an event. And then, what can be an exception to the identitarian system prevalent in every particularity? My answer is: the possibility of multiplicities that are generic and therefore cannot be reduced to an identity. Thinking the universality of a truth becomes a matter of explaining how a generic multiplicity can be constructed within a determinate, particular context without having to go outside that context. On that score, I have no choice but to say that mathematics is crucial, as it has been at various other watershed moments in philosophy. To my mind, the theory of generic multiplicities – one of the mathematician Paul Cohen's discoveries – is as philosophically crucial as differential calculus was for Leibniz or Eudoxian geometry was for Plato, and, in any case, applied to approximately the same problem, namely, how universality can be expressed, articulated, and constructed in an irreducibly particular context.

PP: *I understand the idea that universal truths are ultimately processes of creation for Alain Badiou and that the conditions of access to the universal can therefore not be dependent on the notion of "origin" or even of "destination." I understand the ideas of dispersive ontology and systematic ontology, but what I don't get is how this is connected with the way each of you understands the name "Jew." As far as you're concerned, Jean-Claude Milner, Jews only exist because they call themselves "Jews," and therefore the name "Jew" is the name that takes the status of speaking being to its extreme. We'll get to that. But how is that position really incompatible with Alain Badiou's?*

JCM: Every time I hear Alain Badiou I'm struck by the fact that there's virtually no position that he can't incorporate into his own discourse. I'm exaggerating, of course. Some positions are radically alien, hostile, or inimical to him. But take, for example, a critical position regarding the universal as it functions in most of the established theories: it's clear that Alain Badiou can easily include it as a critical position, that is to say, as a position that presents and points up shortcomings in opinion or conventional theory. In fact, any position with which he enters into a relationship of possible dialogue will come across at the end of that dialogue as one particular case of his *own* theory. That's the hallmark of systemic forms. I can imagine that when an Epicurean argued with a Platonist, the Platonist at some point demonstrated that the Epicurean position was in fact merely a possibility already inscribed in one or another of Plato's dialogues, which, by the way, is quite true. At any rate, let's be aware of this, because it's one of the factors contributing to making our dialogue rather Platonic. In the great Platonic dialogues, the opponent always ends up being assimilated. There's a devouring aspect about the machinery . . .

AB: With regard to the universal, though, I'm actually not so sure . . .

JCM: Well, I hope it isn't sure. The difference between our approaches is perfectly clear, in my opinion. Just as ontology might be said to be the grammar of the verb "to be," I'd say that the theory of the universal as a whole is the grammar of the word "all/whole" [*tout*]. How and under what conditions can this operator be used? Is it used in the singular or in the plural? Is it made into a noun or not? Is it accompanied by the article ("all the," "a whole," and so on) or not? It's not a matter of a pedagogical method; it's more than that: it's the fact that a speaking being can speak. It can speak the universal, using the operator "all/whole," with areas of obscurity that have long been noted but that can be better synthesized today. Is the totality an all-inclusive totality? Is the totality defined by the fact that there's an exception?

I'm referring to the opposition [between the limited all and the unlimited all] that Lacan pointed out. My approach is not at all the same as Badiou's, since I begin with what is said. By the same token, I attach great importance to the fact that the Aristotelian universal starts with the word *holos*, which means "the complete whole," whereas in the Latin translation that became the established one, "universal" refers to the "One" but not to the "whole." On the one hand, you have a word for the universal that makes no mention of the "One" but does mention the "whole": that's the Greek (Aristotelian) approach; and, on the other hand, you have the Latin approach that doesn't mention the "whole" but does mention the "One." The "whole" in this case appears as a sort of horizon that isn't named. Dominating this dual approach, the Christian operation will go beyond the translation of the Greek into Latin to posit their fundamental synonymy in God.

PP: *Still, for you, Jean-Claude Milner, in the same vein as Benny Lévy and his* Le Nom de l'homme *(1984), it's a matter of undermining Saint Paul . . .*

JCM: I was getting to that. When I speak about the Christian operation, I regard it as quite remarkable that the Church should have been defined in Latin as the universal Church and in Greek as the Catholic Church. Nevertheless, I don't equate Saint Paul with the Church. On the contrary, I make a distinction between them. Saint Paul, in my opinion, performed an altogether amazing operation. In order to say that there is neither Greek nor Jew, he proceeded by way of a "We are all 'one' in Jesus Christ." Let's consider that sentence. "We are all one" or "You are all one" starts with the plural "you are," but then the attribute is a "one" in the singular, with the Greek word in the singular. Saint Paul massacred the Greek language here since he ascribed a singular to a plural, which takes some doing, and he massacred Greek logic since he equated "all" (in the plural) with "one." Finally, Saint Paul, Paul of Tarsus, with his highly unusual background, based this operation of conversion of a plural into a singular, of an "all" into a "one," on what was for him the real itself and the impossible itself: the risen Christ.

If we confine ourselves to Saint Paul himself, the universal is *really* impossible. That's why I conclude that to present it as immediately or mediately possible, either here below or in heaven above, either today or tomorrow, is mistaken. I don't think Badiou and I are in deep disagreement over this initial reading of Saint Paul, and in particular over the fact that the pivotal point of the universal is an impossibility – or rather the impossible itself. I think our disagreement comes from somewhere else. It comes from my theory of names, which I don't believe Alain Badiou has an entirely accurate conception of. For me, it is absolutely crucial for the name "Jew" to be a name whose maximal intensity – and here we come back to that opposition between maximal and minimal – depends on its being spoken in the first person.

PP: *The Jews only exist because they call themselves Jews?*

JCM: In the first person. Overall, names exist spoken in the third person. If I'm French, it's because there's a third party, which is called the French state. From its position as the third person, "the French Republic" will validate – or not – the fact that someone can say about you that you're French, the fact that a public official can tell you that you're French, and ultimately the fact that you can say about yourself that you're French. In this case, first-person time and second-person time exist but are logically and temporally posterior to third-person time. In addition, there's a group of names to which I've devoted my activity as a linguist. Where these names are concerned, the initial time isn't third-person but second-person: they are insults.

On this basis a linguistic theory of insults can be constructed, which is something I in fact have done. In Sartre's *Nausea*, the word "bastard" appears in the second person, after the narrator's visit to the museum of Bouville: "Goodbye lovely lilies, goodbye, you Bastards," with a capital "B" in the original [that is, translated] text. I think a category of words, which I'd call second-person words, can be identified this way. In my opinion, the greatness of Sartre's position, in *Réflexions sur la question juive* [translated as *Anti-Semite and Jew*], lies in his having understood that the name "Jew" wasn't a third-person name, as opposed to names of the type "the French" or "the Germans." However, his mistake, the issue on which I part company with him, is that he regarded the name "Jew" as a second-person name. So it's on the lips of the anti-Semite, at the moment when "Jew" comes across as an insult, that the word "Jew" becomes constituted.

For me, the foundational moment of the name "Jew" isn't in the second person but in the first person. This is not the case, as I've said, for the name "French" or for the usual names denoting nationality. Nor is it the case for names denoting religion. At any rate, for the word "Christian" the operation of baptism is necessary: "*ego te baptizo*," "I baptize you," in which can be heard both the giving of a proper name and the entrance into the Christian community. That moment is a sacrament, that is, a Church moment. Even if it depends on the person of the priest, who speaks in the first person (*ego*), even if it's addressed in the second person to the baptized subject (*te*), it's really the third person of the Church that validates the sacrament. What's more, the complete formula reveals who that third person is: *in nomine Patris et Filii et Spiritus sancti*, in the name of the Father, the Son, and the Holy Spirit.

The uniqueness of the name "Jew" is linked to a theory of names. I make a distinction between (1) names whose original time is third-person, with the first- and second-person times being derivatives; (2) names whose original time is second-person, with the other times being derivatives; and (3) the name "Jew," which is the only one that I can mention in Europe today (I stress "today") as being a name whose foundational time is first-person, with the other times being derivatives. My position is effectively related to Benny Lévy's, and the title of his book, *Le Nom de l'homme* [The Name of Man], does indeed refer to something I borrowed – even if I already had my own theory of names and even if the use Benny Lévy makes of the notion of name is peculiar to him.

Of course, my approach to the name "Jew" is such that, at the moment the name is constituted, the universal cannot be tied to it through an "all" in the plural. Indeed, the plural "all" has not been constituted yet. I'm referring to my theory of the speaking being that silences the others. If there is universality, at that moment, it can only be an intensional universality – the type of universality that's obtained when you interpret "every man is mortal" not as a synonym of "all men are mortal" but rather in terms of the most intensional fulfillment in man of that which makes him a man.

AB: To take things from the same starting point again, I'm completely won over by the Greek-Latin-Christian trinitarian theory: first, the universal in its connection with the totality; then, the universal in its connection with the One; and finally, the universal connected to the merging of the One and the totality, that "One Whole" which I was always surprised to see that Deleuze claimed about Spinoza. I'm particularly won over by this trinity since I have no choice but to conclude, not without satisfaction, that I've created a fourth time! For the obvious and immediately apparent reason that in my thinking the universal is unrelated to either the One or the Whole.

First of all, and this is a proposition of the utmost importance in my work, totality doesn't exist. It is the impossibility proper of multiplicity as such. Second of all, being is not related to the One, precisely because the very fabric of ontology is multiplicity without the One. As a result, subjective incorporation into a truth procedure, *qua* universal, is always in the first person. It can only be in the first person since it can't be based on either the Whole or the One. Indeed, "I'm a communist," for example, can only be said in the first person, except, of course, if the thing was re-totalized after the fact by a Church or its equivalent. But if one is still in the Pauline temporality of things, it will be expressed in the first person.

The fact that subjects included in or incorporated within a universal procedure appear to the extent that they declare themselves in the first person is a feature of the universal itself. In this regard, I've always accepted and maintained that there's a clear connection between Jewish identity and the universal. The fact of the matter is that there's this major feature, which is that the name "Jew" is ultimately expressed in the first person, and Jean-Claude Milner very clearly pointed this out and demonstrated it. This means that, in the mediation of the subjective as such, the word "Jew" certainly has a unique position in the dialectic of the universal. This is obviously one of the reasons why Paul, in his time, could only appear in the Jewish world and always mentions this belonging to it as a source of pride.

PP: *Can "position" and "exception" be synonymous?*

AB: Everything hinges on knowing what "Jew" is the exception to. Well, it's an exception to the fact that the speaking of nationality or even of religion is expressed in the third person and represents an incorporation into an established totality: the state or the Church. Historically, "Jew" has always raised an objection to the state. That's the reason why, from the nineteenth century on, so many Jews were involved in communist thought and action, which proclaim the principle of the withering away of the state. That's really why the attempt to give the word "Jew" a basis in the state again, to declare the existence of a "Jewish state," poses so many serious problems, and to so many Jews first of all.

JCM: I don't have the feeling that what's going on here is my being assimilated by Alain Badiou but rather something like a possible consonance between two pieces of music in different keys. Maybe a more accurate consideration of my theses, too. In a recent book that Alain Badiou co-wrote with Éric Hazan (*Reflections on Anti-Semitism*, 2011; English translation 2013), the way he presented my position didn't do justice to the fact that this first-person moment, in the case of the name "Jew," is all-important for me. The notion of "first-person moment" implies that the subject/predicate division, inherited from Aristotle and the Greeks, is not operative. With that division, you begin with a subject that's posited as a subject, then you add predicates to it. With "I'm a Jew" it's *"Jew"* that marks the emergence of the subject and retroactively constitutes the "I." It's the opposite of the predicative scheme. That's my first comment.

My second comment, which is very important for me, goes back to a question I'm tempted to answer in a certain way, without being absolutely set on it. Would Alan Badiou say "I'm a communist" using the name "communist" as a first-person name? Let's assume that's the case. It's clear to me that he wouldn't say "I'm a socialist" (I don't mean the Socialist Party of Martine Aubry here but the designation "socialist" the way Lenin used it when he founded the USSR) in the same way. Why? Because for him there's a communist hypothesis and not – or not any longer – a socialist hypothesis. Likewise, I don't think he'd accept that anyone could say about him or herself "I'm a fascist" using the name "fascist" as a first-person name. Why? Because there's no fascist hypothesis for him and, generally speaking, he could demonstrate that there cannot be such a thing as a fascist hypothesis.

AB: At any rate certainly not a fascist hypothesis in terms of its connection to a founding exception of universality: fascist logic is always identitarian; the generic is its fundamental enemy.

JCM: In Alain Badiou's political position there's a connection between "hypothesis" and "communist" such that any use of the word "communist" in his writing has to be related to the communist hypothesis. The question for me has to do with the first-person utterance of certain political names. I hesitated about this for a long time. I now think – but this is an issue of concrete analysis – that there's no longer any possible use for statements of the type "I'm x or y" with a political name that was originally a first-person name. We come back here to the fact that I don't believe in the possibility of hypotheses – in Badiou's sense of the word – that are political in nature. And that's a fundamental disagreement between us.

PP: *Hence "the politics of things"?*

JCM: If, as I assume, there's no place for first-person names in politics, then things would be all set to reign supreme. Of course, there's the lurking threat of deception: the deception involved in the politics of things consists in acting as if things could speak and say, "I want, I order, I forbid." For example, "the markets are confident," "the markets are wary," and so on. In short, speaking beings are first told: "You can't refer to yourself politically in the first person," to which is then added: "But things can do it for you." I state the first proposition, but I'm careful not to go on to the second one. The politics of things isn't a hypothesis for me, and, if it were to be one, I mean in Badiou's sense, it would be an atrocious hypothesis. Let's be clear. There's no logical contradiction in considering that one can say "I'm a communist" in the first person and that that time is foundational. There's no logical contradiction, but I don't think it's possible in reality.

PP: *Nevertheless, and maybe you'll both agree about this, it's probably easier for you to speak about "difficult universality"[2] than to oppose the politics of things, isn't it?*

JCM: Generally speaking, my criticisms are plentiful and my positive assertions are few and far between.

PP: *And would you say that Alain Badiou is a proponent of "difficult universality"?*

JCM: After listening to him, I can at least appreciate that his theory of universality takes greater account of the difficulties of universality than I had assumed. To come back to what I was saying, if I don't think saying something like "I'm a communist" in a foundational first-person time is possible, that goes hand-in-hand with the fact that I don't think there's any place for

[2] "Difficult universality" (*l'universel difficile*) is the paradoxical universality that is based on difference rather than sameness. "All men are mortal" can be considered an "easy universality" of the extensional type, allowing for the constitution of the class of human beings, whereas "difficult universality," taking mortality to its maximal intensionality, concerns the class of speaking beings. For a partial discussion of this concept, see Jean-Claude Milner, "Une conversation sur l'universel," *Cahiers d'études lévinassiennes* 6 (2007): 77–91.

hypotheses, in the sense that Alain Badiou means it, in politics.

AB: If there's a disagreement here, there's also a disagreement about the word "politics" itself. In "the politics of speaking bodies" or "the politics of things," "politics" strikes me as being purely metaphorical. A politics, for me, is a truth procedure. It is therefore always expressible in the first person, with regard to either a real process, or a hypothesis, or other subjective configurations, but in any case it can be expressed in the first person. If nothing political can be expressed in the first person it's because there's no politics. In line with his condemnation of any "political worldview," Jean-Claude Milner is firmly convinced that politics, in the sense that I mean it, doesn't exist.

JCM: Alain Badiou ascribed that position to me quite a while ago and I had no objection to it.

AB: Whereas I think that politics exists, but in a regime of subjectivation that's weakened today, which is exactly what "hypothesis" denotes.

JCM: At one time, the notion of rarity was associated with politics in Badiou's and a few other people's discourses – I'm thinking of Sylvain Lazarus.[3]

AB: Broadly speaking, truth procedures are rare since they're rooted in an exception to the empirical laws of the world. "Hypothesis" denotes a particular mode of political rarity in the contemporary world.

[3] French sociologist, anthropologist, and political theorist, Sylvain Lazarus (b.1943) wrote, among other works, *L'Anthropologie du nom* (The Anthropology of the Name, 1966), a book on which Badiou drew heavily in his own *Metapolitics* and discussed at some length as well in *Logics of Worlds*. Lazarus is also referenced in Milner's *Les Noms indistincts*.

JCM: I do in fact think that that's an old point of disagreement between us concerning politics. That said,
each of us has gone on working. *Logics of Worlds*
(2006; English translation 2009) puts forward new
propositions with respect to *Being and Event* (1988;
English translation 2006). In subsequent writings of
mine I've added clarifications to what I said in *Constat*
(1992). This is only normal. And even if I've thought
for a relatively long time that there's no such thing as
politics in the sense that Alain Badiou means it, I did
have some hesitation about it. For example, my assertion that there's no such thing as a political hypothesis,
hence no such thing as a communist hypothesis (in the
sense that Badiou means "hypothesis"), is a conclusion
that developed over time, just as the notion of hypothesis itself developed over time. Now, the consequence of
rejecting the possibility of political hypotheses is that
political assertions, even if they may appear to be first-
person assertions, are not in the first person. Third-
person time is generally the original time, with the
exception of when the role is played by second-person
time.

AB: Just to be clear about this, I'd say that if political
assertions are reduced to being in the third person,
they're not political assertions but statist assertions.

JCM: Absolutely, and if politics is in the third person,
that amounts to saying that it's on the horizon of the
state that all this is situated and articulated – but the
state in the broad sense of the term, which exceeds
the notion of state as it's usually meant by legal experts
and sociologists. That's why the notion of third person
is more appropriate. I also said that, in some rare
instances, what appears to be a political assertion begins
with a second-person assertion. I'm among those who
think, not with regard to Nazism in general but to
Hitler in particular, that he began with a second-person

assertion about the Jews – a pure and simple insult. On that basis there later developed a politics that would be expressed in the third person. I have no doubt that there was a Nazi politics and that it involved the state in both the narrow and broad senses of the term.

AB: Insofar as the primordial, Hitlerian Nazi assertion was in the second person, it resembled a political assertion formally. I agree with you that Nazism was not strictly reducible to the third person. But the fundamental issue is that its identitarian essence was a barrier to any universality and precluded political subjectivation in the element of truth. In the end, the only reality of Nazism was indeed the state, in the guise of war and extermination.

PP: *Let's take things from a different angle. The universal in a traditional sense is being countered by identity dynamics today. The self-segregation movement is growing stronger, and not just from a religious or communitarian point of view. This self-segregation is not the end of the story, however. In spite of everything, it is informed by what might be called a "global political awareness" affecting the destiny of future generations as much as climate and the environment.*

JCM: I mentioned the fact that the universal operates as if it conveyed its own self-evidence and clarity and that, in my view, this operation is illegitimate. I'd add that the physical space in which the universal appears as something taken for granted, as conveying its own self-evidence and clarity, is also a space in which the universal appears as something desirable. The universal is not just deemed to be clear in and of itself there; it is also demanded. Yet the space of the demand for the universal is a limited space, not necessarily a desirable one, whose intentions are in some respects only too obvious. Just as, for theoretical reasons, it's not

self-evident that the term "universal" is clear and distinct in itself, it is not self-evident that the demand for
the universal itself has the legitimacy it claims to have.

PP: *No doubt, but does that suffice to explain the ubiq-
uity of the category of the human today? It can be found
in the work of François Jullien, the anthropologists,
obviously, and all those who haven't given up interro-
gating human figures.*

JCM: If I'm right in thinking that what passes for universal purports to define itself as something operating
always and everywhere, not just always and everywhere
now but always and everywhere until the end of time,
then the universal, in my view, is the politics of things.

PP: *OK, but you've read Sartre and Foucault and you're
no mere humanist, as far as I know, right? Does the
"name of man" resonate with your thinking?*

JCM: If the name of man cannot be used in the first
person except as a platitude, then that name is of no
importance whatsoever in my approach. I note what is
being said; in fact, that's my starting point. What I call
politics is the fact of speaking politics. If we confine
ourselves to observation, political speaking is present in
a number of places in the world. I'm not saying that it's
present everywhere: it can be prevented or prohibited.
But where it *is* present, it involves division. This is what
I said at the beginning of our discussions: politics begins
with the suspension of killing – in other words, speaking
rather than killing. This assumes that division haunts
politics; it is only on that condition that there can be
any real avoidance of killing.

Consequently, a name is political, in my usage, to the
precise extent that it divides. The more deeply it divides,
the more political it is. Since the name of man is used
to convey something along the lines of "Let's forget our

divisions. Can't we all just get along, people?" it is not a political name. I'm not the only one who says this, either. Carl Schmitt said as much, for detestable purposes, of course, but Althusser also did. His anti-humanism was an affirmation of politics, reduced to its fundamental divisiveness. In contrast, when people talk about the human and man and claim to be speaking politics, what they're really saying is "Shut the hell up about politics."

AB: I think we need to make a distinction between the possible functions of the words "man" and "human" and what I call "the human animal." The human animal has no special interest when it comes to politics or when it comes to any truth, moreover, because "human animal" denotes the multifaceted substructure of all things. It's simply the way things are. It can, however, be argued that something like man or the human exists when there's a subjective figure. And there's a subjective figure whenever there's a truth procedure. So "the human," or "man," are words denoting the capacity to be incorporated into a truth procedure. If there's no such thing as political truth, there's no sense in using the words "man" or "human." There's nothing but the statized turmoil of human animals, in the configuration of the various material and symbolic orders by which they're structured. On the other hand, if politics exists, it's another matter altogether.

PP: *So you'd agree with Jean-Claude Milner about humanism being doomed?*

AB: There's no generic figure of man; that issue's been settled. There are only (human) subjects of specific truths. So I agree with Jean-Claude Milner when he says that when people talk about man and the human without considering what truth procedure they're referring to, they're actually saying not just "Don't talk about politics" but also "Don't bug us about things like art, science, or love." But maybe France, this exhausted old country, isn't the right observation point today from which to ascertain the real becoming of truths, whatever they may be, and therefore to learn where we stand in terms of the degree of existence of man and humanism, as a subjective figure where the former is concerned and as a doctrine of universal truths where the latter is concerned.

JCM: We'd actually be better off using as an observation point a place where decisions are made. Decisions are made in Beijing, São Paulo, Mumbai, and elsewhere, but definitely not in Paris. I've said on occasion that French is a dead language. This goes hand-in-hand with the fact that few decisions are made in it – or let's go even further and say that it's becoming the language of non-decision.

AB: I think the only possible way of restoring a sphere of decision-making for our current observation point is a pure and simple fusion of France and Germany.

JCM: That's an old theory of Badiou's, which comes up against the problem of languages – and not just that . . .

AB: Incidentally, I was really surprised to read that Michel Serres[4] is a strong advocate of the idea of such a fusion. That could be the basis of a very unusual united front. As for the issue of languages, we've got the example of Switzerland right before our eyes. In any case, this would be a way for us to rebuild a real power base.

---

[4] Michel Serres (b. 1930), the author of numerous books and essays, is a prominent French philosopher and a member of the Académie française. In addition to teaching at the University of Paris, he has been a Professor of French at Stanford University since 1984.

JCM: And there was someone – I hardly dare say this – who understood that: Napoleon. Basically, that was what the project of the Continental Blockade was, namely, to extend from the Atlantic coast to the borders of Russia.

AB: I've even got to admit – and this is even less my natural affinity than Napoleon could ever be – that there was something similar about the De Gaulle–Adenauer alliance.

JCM: Absolutely. Except that Adenauer really stood for the left bank of the Rhine: he wanted nothing to do with Prussia, including for religious reasons. He clearly played the division of Germany card, there's no doubt about that. Adenauer's essential defeat was the reunification of Germany, which was, incidentally, a defeat of Gaullism, too.

PP: *What about you, Jean-Claude Milner? Would you tend to agree with Alain Badiou about this idea of uniting France and Germany?*

JCM: Yes, in the abstract, like an intellectual fancy. I wouldn't even call it a hypothesis.

AB: Neither would I. It's just a regulative notion.

JCM: The catastrophe that befell Europe, and indeed the whole world, was a result of Bismarck's decision to tamper with the 1815 borders. German unification didn't need it. The influence of science was decisive in that instance: I have in mind the German linguists and historians who constantly demonstrated, with proofs and arguments to back them up, that French unity was a fiction. Not only would Alsace and a part of Lorraine return to the fold of the German language, they predicted, but, as a result of the French defeat, the France of the langue d'Oïl and the France of the langue d'Oc [the main dialects – Oïl in the north, Oc in the south – spoken in medieval France] would separate from each other. They were proven wrong, but a mechanism had been put in place, and it was responsible for two world wars.

I have no objection to Badiou's proposition as he formulates it. But if you consider the empirical reality and leave the question of language aside, the obstacle, as I see it, would come from the neo-Bismarckianism lurking in it, which is also based on a science or a so-called science. It's not linguistics or history anymore but economics. If the experts in that field are to be believed, France, within a Franco-German union, would become a dominion, as Poland is in the process of becoming. That's hardly an attractive proposition.

But let's leave that aside. I want to go back to our discussion about humanism. Beneath the proliferation of references to man, the human, humanism, humanitarianism, and so forth, there's a real issue – that of potential killing. Think about Syria in the summer of 2012. The incipient shift in public opinion that emerged at the time had to do with the killing, the images of killing. The words "man" and "human" suddenly intruded into public opinion like seemingly positive terms, but in fact they didn't refer to any specific reality. The real persisted in the guise of a question, not an assertion: is individual or mass murder legal or illegal, legitimate or illegitimate? That question *was* real.

PP: *With regard to that question, can you compare the way each of you has reacted to the various military interventions that have occurred since the one in Kuwait? Some of them were decided on by the UN; others, such as the one in Libya, weren't. Alain Badiou has been consistent in his almost blanket condemnation of these interventions, including the one in the former Yugoslavia. What would you say today about Syria, Jean-Claude*

*Milner? The war ravaging that country is often pre-
sented as an ethnic or religious conflict, whereas there
have recently been – in June 2012 – targeted political
assassinations among many families of intellectuals,
doctors, and others. What's your opinion about these
assassinations?*

JCM: Earlier we noted that, for me, there's no politics
in the sense that Alain Badiou means it. If politics has
any meaning for me, a meaning beyond the purely conversational, it has to do with one minimal distinctive
feature: politics begins from the moment when the
killing of the adversary is, so to speak, beyond the pale.
I didn't invent that definition. You can find it in Guizot's
De la peine de mort en matière politique (1822) or in
Hannah Arendt's work. I make no claim whatsoever to
originality. That being the case, killing cannot be the
way to win a political victory. This means that political
assassination is a contradiction in terms. That's the
starting point.

The second step is that, in both public opinion and
theory, keeping to the minimum is rare. One of the most
common viewpoints involves defining politics as the
conquest or preservation of state power. If politics is
understood that way, then all *de facto* powers, with few
exceptions, carry out political assassination more or less
overtly. If you think about France, the period of the war
in Algeria abounded in political assassinations. I'm
including the *ratonnades* [racist attacks on suspected
FLN members in the Algerian Muslim community]. In
recent years, inasmuch as France has become less geo-
graphically ambitious, there have been fewer occasions
for carrying out political assassinations, but as soon as
a country reaches a certain size or deems that its own
survival is at stake, the issue comes back. At one time,
West Germany regarded itself as sufficiently threatened
by the Red Army Faction (RAF) to engage in conduct
that was a lot like political assassination vis-à-vis the

imprisoned RAF leaders – and all because, at that time, West Germany was afraid of disappearing, of being swallowed up by the Soviet empire. In the opinion of people who are well informed about the United States, the possibility of political assassination is ever-present there; it's no accident that so many TV productions and movies use it as the basis for their plots. The same is true for Russia and many other countries, which it's unnecessary to list.

I'll just note here that political assassination is extremely widespread. That does not alter the fact that it is the negation of politics or, if you prefer, that politics exists to ensure that killing is not one of its means. This is why outrage about killings cannot be limited to an outburst of compassion; it must have a political significance. Sometimes people who are outraged are aware that politics itself is at stake. Every instance of killing is an expression of the fact that politics has ceased to exist – for the time being or forever, it makes little difference.

Be that as it may, outrage is the most fairly distributed thing in the world; that is, no one thinks they should feel more outraged than they actually do. I'm borrowing Descartes's aphorisms about common sense here – they apply perfectly. This also means that outrage is always partial, hence selective. And, finally, it means that everyone assesses the occasion for and degree of their outrage in terms of their own imaginary. But I'll also draw on another of Descartes's aphorisms, this one concerning the passions: outrage is always "all good."[5] It so happened that Libya provoked the outrage of a few people, or perhaps, in the beginning, of only one person, Bernard -Henri Lévy. Gaddafi carried out political assassinations on a grand scale, yet every political assassination should

---

[5] Cf. "We see that they [the passions] are all good in their nature and that we have nothing to avoid but their evil uses or their excesses." Descartes, *The Passions of the Soul*, xi, 485.

provoke outrage. This outrage *qua* outrage is "all good." Insofar as it refers to the minimal definition of politics, it can be "all political." It's just that what can be observed (but this goes with the territory) is that such outrage is circumstantial. And in fact it can always be argued that similar things, which no one says a word about, are happening in other places, but that's inevitable. To say "Be outraged" without specifying the day and the place amounts to preaching. To say "Be outraged," specifying the day and the place, amounts to being selective. So, yes, a few people were outraged about Libya, and Nicolas Sarkozy, the president at the time, saw fit to join in that outrage. From that moment on, it became a matter of state policy, and it will be judged as such.

Between subjective outrage and state politics there is always a gap, necessarily. States don't judge things in terms of outrage; they judge in terms of their own interests. The fact that they use a few people's subjective outrage as a pretext doesn't devalue the outrage per se. I can be outraged about the state's duplicity, but I'm not outraged about the outrage.

PP: *Alain Badiou, are you outraged about the outrage?*

AB: I totally disagree with the idea that politics begins when you say that political assassination is always a bad thing. Obviously, the expression "political assassination" is already off-putting enough. You immediately feel like you're in the world of Racine's Nero. What's more, "political assassination" is an expression that's associated with the register of the state far more than with that of collective political action. If you're speaking about the need to defend yourself when you've achieved a dominant position or about the need to recognize that there are traitors and collaborators, if you're speaking in actual situations, then that moralizing discourse is totally bogus. Violence is not and has never been a critical issue of politics. Like virtually everyone – except for fascists and a few adherents of certain variants of *gauchisme* – I want politics to avoid violence, but I don't think that such a desire could be changed into an axiom. My position is the same as Mao's: we don't want war, but if the enemy forces it on us, then we won't be afraid of it.

Now for outrage. Atrocities do occur in the contemporary world. In general, they aren't perceived from within a true political framework of judgment. They're perceived at the basic level of compassion for distant human animals who are overwhelmingly the victims of various catastrophes. Outrage, from this point of view, is legitimate, but uninformed. And what's appalling, apart from the atrocities themselves, is the instrumentalization of this uninformed compassion by the powerful countries, which intervene militarily so as to pursue objectives that have nothing to do with the atrocities. These objectives involve setting up zones where countries and big corporations can blithely go about the economic looting that is the only thing that interests them. The objectives of these powerful countries almost always compound the misfortunes of the populations in question with other endless atrocities, as can clearly be seen in both Iraq and Afghanistan, in the Ivory Coast as in Libya, in Congo, and in Haiti.

PP: *What about Syria?*

AB: I'm not sure about Syria. I note that the powerful countries are in a real quandary about what the most advantageous plan of action would be with regard to the situation. This incidentally proves that it's not at all the atrocities or outrage that motivates them but rather that, whatever the situation, they are the coldest of cold monsters, as Nietzsche perceptively observed. So they should not be given any powers of moral policing.

JCM: The proof of this is the hesitation being shown by Russia, which is objectively the dominant power in the region. The fact that it can be imagined for one moment that Russia might change its position, while the nature of Russian power can hardly be said to have changed, is a sign. A sign of what? Of uncertainty, where the dominant power is concerned, about the outcome of calculations of self-interest. But I'd like to go back to the minimal definition I gave of politics. This is a very important point of disagreement. So I need to say more about it, in particular about the issue of killing itself. It's a key issue and deserves to be unpacked.

It can be approached from two different yet complementary angles: the one I mentioned before – politics as putting the death of the adversary beyond the pale – but also the one that Max Weber implicitly pointed out. In *Le Savant et le politique* (1919; two lectures translated as "Politics as a Vocation" and "Science as a Vocation") he defined the state as having a monopoly on legitimate physical violence. I interpret this to mean legitimate killing. All things considered, this is not just a definition of the state but, in a very real sense, a delimitation of politics.

As so defined, the state appears as the limit form of politics: the outer limit, since it can kill and thus places itself beyond politics, and the inner limit, since, by reserving to itself the monopoly on killing, it constitutes the field from which killing is excluded. In that sense, it belongs to politics. This comes down to saying that the relationship between the state and politics is always a problematic one. Badiou and I will agree on that. But we'll stop agreeing when it comes to the *reason* the relationship is problematic. In my view, the state makes politics possible by reserving to itself what makes it impossible. Insofar as it makes politics possible, it determines the geometrical locus, as it were, of political statements. But, by the same token, it is always in the process of embodying the negation of politics.

If you consider major historical events, and I think we'd agree about including the French Revolution in that category, this was a crucial issue. And hesitation was crucial, too. It was epitomized by Robespierre. He opposed war and the death penalty precisely because politics, in his opinion, put killing beyond the pale. He was nevertheless prepared to admit that there were circumstances in which killing was legitimate, but those circumstances had to be as rare as possible. In fact, they had to be exceptional.

It was because the king had placed himself beyond politics, and it was ultimately because any king *qua* king excepts himself from politics, that Louis XVI could – and had to – be executed. Then, as a result of the necessities associated with the war and the Terror, which was to a great extent a consequence of the war, the exception became the rule. Killing was transformed into a government procedure, a rule of state. The state thus became increasingly necessary to the possibility of politics, to the point of appropriating politics and changing it into its opposite. A good many historians think that Robespierre consented to his own downfall. I could readily assume that he drew the necessary conclusions from a failure – a titanic failure, to borrow Virginia Woolf's comment about Joyce. Before his very eyes and as a result of his own actions, politics had ceased to exist.

AB: Needless to say, we should adhere to the maxim "It is better not to kill, if possible." I always make a distinction between politics and the state, and, when I say that politics can be armed with the closely monitored and controlled principle "it is better not to kill," I know that that doesn't absolutely guarantee that it will be so, because politics is antagonistic, and because there are states. So the camp of emancipatory, or communist, politics is not the only one that decides. As Jean-Claude Milner quite aptly remarked about Robespierre, and as the experiment of the socialist states has passed the experience on to us, killing doesn't resolve problems, because, as a rule, killing creates the impression that the problem has gone away; it doesn't create the real of the problem's solution.

JCM: I share Alain Badiou's view about what he calls "antagonistic." After all, "antagonistic," the term he uses, only reiterates in Greek what's expressed, for me, by the Latin term "adversarial." Someone who thinks that politics makes killing their adversary illegitimate can't be sure that their adversary has the same mindset. In political warfare, this conception of politics is not necessarily shared by both sides.

There are adversaries who are anti-political. Take the Spanish Civil War, for instance. If I go back to Bernanos's book *The Great Cemeteries Under the Moon* [also known as *A Diary of My Times*], it's clear that the Republicans were involved in politics and that their adversaries were beyond politics. It goes without saying that when a political struggle is waged, it's not self-evident that the opposing sides will both put killing beyond the pale.

PP: *Can each of you explain what you mean by "political decision"? This expression is found more often in Jean-Claude Milner's writing than in Alain Badiou's. Political decisions necessarily lead to there being a difference between those who make them and those who don't. They are related to disillusionment with democratic speech, because to speak out in a democracy is not the same as to make political decisions, as we see quite clearly all the time.*

JCM: When I said that decisions were made elsewhere, I was opening the possibility that there could be a wide variety of decisions that aren't political in the strict sense of the term. In common usage, whatever lays claim to the word "political" is political, regardless of whether it's in actual fact political or not. I don't feel bound by that usage.

PP: *But political decisions are related to power; they . . .*

JCM: If we confine ourselves to common usage, everything decided by state power – both executive and legislative – is a political decision; only what's decided by state power is a political decision. In my approach, I accept the relationship between politics and the state, even if, as I have argued, that relationship is disharmonic or even contradictory. To simplify the debate, I will therefore accept that what's decided by state power is sometimes a political decision. But it's not true that everything so decided is a political decision.

Let me give a very banal example. Switching from a majority voting system in legislative elections to a proportional system is generally regarded as a political decision. That decision will be widely discussed and argued about, but, as I see it, the consequences will only be very minor. Sure, there will be more representatives from minority factions, but I regard that as a mere detail compared with what I consider to be political. It seems clear to me that, over the whole spectrum of what we agree to dub "political," the decisions made in a country like France have relatively limited political consequences.

AB: The term "political decision" is a bit fuzzy because it doesn't make clear the distinction between decision of state and political decision. If we wanted to clarify the meaning of "political" in "political decision" a little, we'd say that we're always dealing with decisions of state and that the question of whether or not something is a political decision concerns collective subjectivity in one way or another, or the type of collective subject to which we're referring when politics is being spoken about. It's the subjective resonance of the decision that will make it possible to call it a political decision and to distinguish it more or less from power decisions or statist decisions, which are innumerable and very often not well known.

JCM: I realize that. But you've got to acknowledge the fact that that in many, let's say European, countries, a good political decision, i.e., a decision that legitimately deserves to be called political, can be recognized by the fact that it changes the fewest things possible, in keeping with the spirit of democracy.

AB: Yes, absolutely. That was, incidentally, the big slogan of Edgar Faure, a politician of the Fourth Republic: "Inertia is on the move and nothing can stop it!" Basically, power is not in the business of making political decisions. Decisions of state exist, hidden more often than not, and disguising them as political decisions is above all a rhetorical activity, a promotional activity. Just look at the meaning the word "change" has taken on. Change has become the key electoral category. Every candidate proclaims: "A vote for me is a vote for change."

4

The Right, the Left, and France in General

PP: *Between the socialist idea as it developed from Saint-Simon to Jaurès in the nineteenth century and today's social democracy, which has seriously compromised itself with neoliberalism, there's a wide gap that is unlikely to shrink any time soon. To define its scope, let me first ask Alain Badiou a question. In an interview from 1995 entitled "Les Échecs de Mitterrand [Mitterrand's failures],"[1] you stressed the fact that the basis of François Mitterrand's staying power was always the way he exhausted his own supporters. That's what you called at the time "consensus governmentality," which was underpinned by a figure of the real pervaded by death. As compared with that analysis, what would you say today about the new governmentality implemented by François Hollande? What would you say about the so-called "normal" candidate?*

AB: Since 1980–90 I've expanded my analysis of the parliamentary category of "the left." In 1981 and the

[1] See Alain Badiou, *Entretiens 1: 1981–1996* (Paris: Nous, 2011), 203–222.

years following, I and my friends from the UCFML [Marxist-Leninist Union of Communists of France, 1969–85] and later from the Organisation politique [1985–2007] needed to distance ourselves right away from the festive consensus that had greeted Mitterrand, the presidential candidate. We had to demonstrate our dissidence, which was very much a minority position, vis-à-vis the pathetic "We won!" atmosphere of the times. I have since analyzed in greater depth the historico-political, and rather typically French, concept of "the left." I understood – I discussed this new understanding in *Circonstances 7*, a short book published in 2012 – to what extent the left, particularly in our country, represents what I call an "Idea" in my philosophical language.

Yes, the left is more than a parliamentary political faction, more than a fluctuating ideological trend, more than a form of criticism. It's an Idea. This explains its resilience and its ongoing presence. It also explains a very curious phenomenon, namely, the public's indifference to the left's failures and turpitude. The fact that nothing it says it will do ever comes to pass, that it backs down at the slightest obstacle, that it carefully follows in the footsteps of the right, and so on – none of that ever impinges on the continued existence and periodic return to power of this parliamentary zombie. Indeed, an Idea can survive its most pathetic incarnations.

PP: *What's the substance of this Idea?*

AB: I suggest that the left, in our country, is an artificial synthesis between ordinary parliamentary consensus – hence, keeping capitalist phenomena just as they are – and a tradition with its own principles, folklore, and images, which can easily tolerate its obvious powerlessness. This tradition is made up of republican borrowings from the French Revolution, socialistic borrowings from the late nineteenth century, and a mishmash of disjointed references to Marx, Proudhon, Jaurès, et al. The "left" stands for the idea that there can be a synthesis between this largely folkloric tradition – which ultimately took the name "the left" after first adopting a few others – and the consensus governing all the Western "democracies" today, a pro-capitalistic consensus that tolerates only very minor deviations.

The left comes to power in the brief periods of subjective exhaustion of the right, namely, when the situation is such that the consensus has to be rebuilt and certain strata of the population that had fallen away from it have to be won over again. Sarkozy ran roughshod over the power elite and the official state bodies [*corps constitués*], insulted the left's folklore, worshipped the rich, reunited the Atlantic Alliance, and scorned French literature, which is a sacred cow in our country. In the process, he inspired a dangerous loathing of himself, if not of the regime that condoned his misconduct. When it comes to bringing these angry social groups back into the fold, nothing beats a good dose of the left.

Given all this, I can answer your question. The "normal" candidate strikes me as being a normal man of the left. And I think it will all be business as usual. In the beginning, a few measures will be taken to show that what's involved is indeed a synthesis between the progressive, emancipatory, republican, revolutionary, democratic tradition and the "deplorable" situation that was inherited from the right. There will be long, fruitless "consultations with social partners." And finally the time will come for a return to serious matters – the ones having to do with capitalist competition – with the inevitable implementation of an austerity plan. In 1983 that plan was rather elegantly dubbed "the austerity turn" [*le tournant de la rigueur*]. To date, I have no idea what ingenious phrase will be used this time around. Ingenious phrases are very important for the left because, as the synthesis it lays claim to is a sham, it always has to be made to exist in words. "*Le tournant de la rigueur*" wasn't bad. But will Hollande's prose be even more creative? We'll find out soon enough.

PP: *"Don't look too far ahead; life is more intelligent than you are,"* François Mitterrand once said. That *"quiet force" of his didn't stick with him to the end, to judge by the appearance of cadaveric decomposition that you rightly noted about him*[2] *but which can't serve as an interpretive framework for his first seven-year term and his legacy today.*

AB: I was obviously talking about the Mitterrand of 1995, when Mitterrandism was on its last legs, and the symbol of which was death invading the body of the president himself. Today, we're not going to have any of the unique phenomena of Mitterrandism, neither the depressing initial enthusiasm for it nor its horrific decline. All we'll have, so to speak, is the synthetic emptiness of the Idea. All we'll have is the austerity turn, under some new name that will be – or so our love of languages can hope – an ingenious phrase worthy of the left's eternal facticity.

JCM: Mitterrand is a special case for a lot of reasons, and I'm not going to go back over them. Rightly or wrongly, I have the feeling he's been forgotten. I don't know whether this forgetting is permanent or not, but whatever it is, it's fine with me. Overall, I just want to add a few tweaks to all the comments that have been made.

---

[2] "*La force tranquille*" ("the quiet force") was Mitterrand's campaign slogan in 1981. In the same year, he was diagnosed with inoperable cancer, but this was kept a state secret until 1992. His ghastly appearance and obvious decline in the last year or so of his life left no doubt that he was close to death. See Badiou's "Les Échecs de Mitterrand," pp. 218–220 in particular, for a fuller discussion of the relationship between Mitterrand's policies and death.

My first comment is that the terms "right" and "left" only make sense in a parliamentary context. I see no reason to extend their use, especially since such language didn't become established in *all* parliamentary systems, particularly not in Great Britain or the US. Those exceptions are significant enough for us to be wary about giving too much weight to the right/left opposition.

My second comment is that there are no left-wing values that can be opposed to right-wing ones, in my opinion. To be on the left is to vote for someone or some party that calls itself left-wing; ditto for the right.

My third comment is that, little by little, the idea has taken hold in France that you can say you're on the left but that you can't safely say you're on the right. The left has become the only label that can be claimed by the people affiliated with it. The "right-wing" label is one that's stuck on you by an opponent. The philosopher Alain, who was a member of the Radical Party, had already observed this, in the 1930s, I believe. Let me quote from memory: "When someone starts out by saying 'I'm not on the right, but . . . ,' I conclude that he's on the right." The process by which someone ends up being labeled as a rightist always involves a denial: a person who's on the right can use the word "right," but only if they accompany it with an "I'm not." By the same token, when someone on the left refers to themself, they'll avoid using the word "right" like the plague and especially in a negative way. When a professional politician feels obliged to declare: "I've never been on the right," "I don't feel at home on the right," and so on, they're admitting they've been put on the defensive. There are doubtless some exceptions, but this is a general rule and even, more precisely, a rule of civility.

My fourth comment is that, over the five years of Nicolas Sarkozy's term of office, we observed a determination to shake up that traditional scheme of things.

Having a right that referred to itself as right-wing, along with the emergence of a group calling itself the "Popular Right," was contrary to the practices of the right in general and the Gaullist right in particular. The latter always insisted on not using the word "right" to describe itself – the word "popular," the word "national," yes, but not the word "right." Nicolas Sarkozy flouted convention; such flouting was of a piece with all the gaffes he was criticized for, the "Get lost,"[3] his victory celebration at the chi-chi restaurant Fouquet's, and so on. It revealed that those gaffes were not just oversights or signs of some emotional disturbance, but were part and parcel of a political strategy – which was deemed intolerable.

This explains the total rejection that marked his term of office. Nicolas Sarkozy intentionally disrupted a wide array of arrangements that had long been in place. He thus alienated a large part of the UMP [his own party, the center-right Union for a Popular Movement] apparatus. The issue of the Front National[4] was the visible form of the disruption, but the real issue was whether the right could win back power by referring to itself as right-wing or whether it would instead have to return to the previous set-up, in which the right was not supposed to refer to itself as right-wing. In addition to the rules of language, which are fundamental, there's the objective reality they express. I call this objective reality the "division/reconciliation of the power elite."

For a very long time the French system was based on the division of the power elite. In the nineteenth century they had been divided between Legitimists and

---

[3] "Get lost, you jerk!" (*Casse-toi, pauvre con!*) was Sarkozy's notorious comment to a man who got on his nerves at the Paris Agricultural Fair in 2008.
[4] The increasingly influential Front National, which had already shown surprising strength in the 2002 presidential elections, is a far-right party currently headed by Marine Le Pen, who took over after her father, Jean-Marie Le Pen, retired in 2011.

Orleanists, between royalists and Bonapartists. In the twentieth century they were divided over the issue of collaboration and the Resistance, and over the colonial wars. The division between right and left was seen as a subordinate one at that time. Now, however, it would seem as though that division is the only one left. The counterpart of division is reconciliation in the face of danger, i.e., in the face of social unrest. In 1850, in the shadow of the 1848 revolutions, Adolphe Thiers,[5] who was no fool, stated something that provides the key to the modern French system: "The Republic is the form of government that divides us the least." That "us" is only too clear: "us" is the power elite. Seeking the least divisive form of government was necessary precisely because division was a fact of life and, in an emergency, it had to be put in abeyance. After the Commune, Thiers would remember this notion of establishing a republic as the least divisive form of government.

I'll skip the connection between that model and my own definition of politics. For the time being, I'd just like to highlight an interpretive key for the French government machine: temporary reconciliation against the backdrop of division; temporary reconciliation prompted by fear.

De Gaulle returned to power in 1958, at a time when the power elite, faced with the threat of a military *pronunciamento* and recognizing that the colonial war in Algeria threatened to exclude them permanently from global prosperity, realized that it was time to reconcile. But they couldn't do so on their own. So they turned to the Statue of the Commander – who understood perfectly what was involved. Something similar happened after 1968: in the grip of fear of "the street" (Georges Pompidou's term), the power elite came together on a

---

[5] Adolphe Thiers (1797–1877), a French historian and politician, suppressed the Paris Commune and became a founder and the first president of the Third Republic.

deal that combined getting rid of De Gaulle and accepting the 1958 Constitution. It was in fact then that the left stopped making the rejection of the Constitution a critical litmus test and, with Mitterrand, launched the process of getting into power. It took them longer than expected, but that's a minor detail.

To return to Alain Badiou's analysis, I agree, in my own way, with his idea about the vital importance of rhetorical declaration for the left. Referring to itself as left-wing is what defines it. That necessity is also a privilege. The left is the only political faction that can declare itself positively as a faction. The right can't do so, and it consequently tends to resort to using one person's surname.

To complete my own analysis, I think that there have been two or three attempts during the Fifth Republic to break with the system of reconciliation/division of the power elite, if only because it leads to automatic paralysis – a zero-sum game. Sarkozy went to great lengths to pursue that effort. When he became president, he thought he could count on global prosperity; back then, everyone thought it would last forever. He spoke to the power elite and told them that if they wanted to share in global profit-making they would have to change both their pace and their relationship to making fast money. When the financial crisis hit, he had no positive plan for dealing with it. His only option was to impose his will on the power elite by using the fear of the crisis – in other words, the fear of losing prosperity. In this respect, he was pretty adroit tactically, but he erred strategically. He kept telling the power elite in too blunt a way: "Your time's up; assets are nothing compared with profit. Survival of the fittest is the name of the game."

AB: Hence his ongoing hostility to the established bodies, the so-called intermediary bodies [*corps intermédiaires*, i.e., associations, unions, lobbies, political parties, the media, etc.]. In my opinion, that's what did him in.

JCM: Right. The theme of normality played a part in the campaign; I interpret it as a desire for normalization after the attempt to upset a certain kind of equilibrium. It was a reactive desire for normalization. The people who voted for François Hollande wanted the power elite to come together around a model in which the President of the Republic would be present without being too present; in which the regions would be acknowledged but not to the point where they would undermine national unity; in which, vis-à-vis Germany, which has been playing the neo-Bismarckian card increasingly obviously, the rights of small countries would have to be remembered but without giving up on the idea of France as a great nation, and so on. What will happen in practice is another story.

AB: I'm very broadly in agreement with Jean-Claude Milner. I'm sure international politics is involved in all this, insofar as it's a matter of returning to a balanced approach. That kind of balance is consistent with a "normal" domestic administration, which aims to restore the traditional balances among the prominent republican figures and at the same time to promote a great show of concern for the social safety net, which is part of these overall balances and is moreover a crucial component of the idea of the left. I also agree that Sarkozy's presidency – whose reactionary original-ity I pointed out right from the start – represented a real attempt to do away with these balances.

JCM: A real attempt, sure, but by someone who didn't have a strong enough personality to pull it off. Like-wise, although with far more substantial political personnel, Gaullism, or more precisely De Gaulle's presidency, was also a real attempt, involving, among other things, the dissolution or weakening of a variety of local powers.

AB: And, what's more, the 1969 referendum, which would have eliminated the senate – a referendum De Gaulle lost – had turned every last one of the provincial power elite against him. Giscard d'Estaing, the traitor, the General's minister of finance, had assumed the leadership of that rebellion and reaped the rewards of his betrayal when he beat the Gaullist candidate in the 1974 presidential election.

JCM: In a sense, Sarkozy's loss of the senate was similar to De Gaulle's loss of the 1969 referendum, which in fact had to do with a reform of the senate. As soon as the right realized it was losing control of the senate on account of Sarkozy and his territorial reform project, the alarm bells went off. It wasn't just a question of the right in general and legislative power; it was a question of a certain right, the one I call the patrimonial right, which is based on legacy rather than business, on mayoral rather than ministerial posts – in a nutshell, power elite in the most traditional sense of the term. Of course, the De Gaulle–Sarkozy analogy only goes so far. The possibility of a military coup was very real in 1958, whereas recently . . .

AB: Right, the danger was not the same, after all.

PP: *In that regard, what's left of Sarkozyism, in your opinion?*

JCM: My assumption is that there are still some lobby groups that think the French model has run out of steam. That's a theory believed by a number of people, and, if you take them seriously it means several things, such as, for example, that the right should be able to use the word "right" about itself; that the whole local power elite system should be consigned to oblivion; that the "machines" designed to multiply the power elite should be destroyed – I'm thinking of decentralization; and that French-style collective bargaining should be radically transformed.

It is generally acknowledged that the cornerstone of the French social model is collective bargaining and that the cornerstone of French-style collective bargaining does not consist, as in Germany, of bringing together the employer organization concerned (the metal-working, automobile, chemical industries, and so on) and the industry-wide union concerned. Rather, collective bargaining in France consists of bringing together, under the auspices of the government, high-level government officials and representatives of the big labor union federations. The notion of industry-wide unions and the role of the employer organizations are only secondary, as is – let's face it – the concept of representativeness: the big labor federations and their leaders are no more representative than the high-level officials on the other side of the table. Some Sarkozyists think it's time to put an end to all this. They regard it as a rigged game, because the high-level officials don't have an accurate understanding of capitalist needs, and the unions, with their small numbers, only exist thanks to the consideration given them by the high-level officials.

Sarkozy's presidency did in fact put a different model in place for retirement reform. Under the traditional model, the constant demonstrations, the wholehearted support of public opinion, and commentators' opinions would all have led the government to back down, with the president intervening only as a last resort to calm things down. In the case of the retirement reforms, the president himself, on the strength of his election by direct popular vote, chose to challenge the unions. Would they dare ramp up the mobilization? Would they dare disturb public order? He was sure they wouldn't. And he was right. The change in method was viewed as exceptionally ruthless since it amounted to an outright power play. I'm sure that in some think-tanks that episode is, or will soon become, a model, just as it's a counter-model on the left and for a large part of the right.

I'm sure some think-tanks are going to try and take inspiration from that model and popularize and idealize it. But I predict that they'll have more and more trouble building a constituency for it within the electoral system. I'm obviously not talking about the left, but on the right, provincial politicians and big-city mayors, who don't think in those terms at all, have been making a comeback. The power elite *qua* power elite think that one thing above all needs to be preserved, namely, agreement about the system that put them in the position of being the power elite. Or to put it more bluntly: since they themselves are numerically weak and economically marginal, they don't want to rely on the unions' weakness – they'd run the risk of giving their own secret away. People like Juppé and Fillon [foreign minister and prime minister, respectively, under Sarkozy] do think in such terms. There might be a school of thought that could be called "Sarkozyist," the way there was a Reaganite school of thought in the US, but the Republicans aren't Reaganites today, and the mere fact that there exists a Sarkozyist school of thought certainly doesn't mean that the right will be Sarkozyist.

PP: *In light of this reconstruction and constitutive bipolarity, and in relation to what Alain Badiou calls "the eternal left," what is the situation of the left-wing intellectual today? Jean-Claude Milner, you once said: "Today, the success of the 1981 operation is plain: we don't have left-wing intellectuals, only intellectuals who vote on the left." Is that dictum still relevant?*

JCM: I don't know whether Alain Badiou will agree with this description and analysis, but it does seem to me that the ideal type of left-wing intellectual, at the time of the colonial wars, for example, was embodied by intellectuals who always maintained their activity as intellectuals.

I'll use Sartre as an example. He always maintained his role as an intellectual. He published *Critique of Dialectical Reason* (1960; English translation 1976). When he wrote articles in the newspapers, they weren't journalistic in nature but articles by a philosopher-writer. (*Situations V* [1964; translated as *Colonialism and Neo-Colonialism*, 1976] is impressive in this regard.) Always maintaining his role as an intellectual, he used that role to reorient the discourse of those who called themselves left-wing so that they'd be led to say things they would never have said by themselves. Regarding Algeria, for instance, the left-wing parties' tendency was not to consider the FLN as a dialogue partner or to acknowledge support for the FLN as a practice to be encouraged. But for Sartre in particular and for the left-wing intellectuals in general, to speak to those who called themselves left-wing was necessarily to speak to the parties.

Someone like Alain Badiou always maintains his role as an intellectual as well as his determination to make the left hear things that, in his opinion, they should be saying. Even so, I don't think he's trying to achieve results comparable to the ones Sartre achieved, simply because, for him, the left-wing parties aren't dialogue partners. He doesn't preclude the possibility of being heard by them, but he precludes speaking directly to them. Maybe he'd say that he speaks to subjects who call themselves left-wing in order to reorient their positions and actions, but in so doing he completely disconnects them from the left-wing parties. He's an intellectual, but he's not a left-wing intellectual. At bottom, I wouldn't even say he's on the left since, in my terms, you're on the left if, and only if, you vote on the left. But Badiou has theorized a political course of action that doesn't including voting. So, in my terms, the label "left-wing" doesn't apply to him.

Considering the general case now, there are a lot of intellectuals who vote on the left, hence for a left-wing party. But I don't see any who are attempting to change these parties' choices in any meaningful way – certainly not by using their role as intellectuals.

AB: I do in fact think that if you reconstruct the history of the existence of the left-wing intellectual – something that's another very French concept – it cannot be separated from the joint existence of the socialist party outside our country and a powerful communist party within it. The PCF [French Communist Party] – which, don't forget, garnered about 30 percent of the votes and completely controlled what is by far the largest and best organized union – represented a force within the parliamentary system that nevertheless claimed to be *outside* that system. It was always possible to challenge the PCF's positions on any given issue. It was possible not to care much for the Soviet regime. But both of them sustained the hypothesis that non-consensual forces could exist around the world, on the one hand, and within the French parliamentary system, on the other.

Those forces demonstrated that it was possible for a foreign discourse to be taken up, or to be influential, on the domestic front. Even if you weren't a follower of the Party or the USSR, they stood for the possibility of domestic dissidence, of something genuinely different, which could be put into practice in the capitalist countries in general and in France in particular. The category of fellow-traveler (of the PCF) was rightly promoted. It didn't mean that the fellow-traveler agreed with or used the same language as the PCF or the Soviets; it meant that a road existed and that on that road the direction to be taken could come from what was being said or written by the intellectuals, whose influence was by no means regarded as insignificant.

Our situation is very different today, and I think that the category of left-wing intellectual doesn't have the same meaning anymore, because the left itself doesn't have the same meaning anymore. There is certainly something that I called the "eternal left," but the practical existence of this "eternal left" is periodized in widely varying situations. When people were just emerging from the Resistance and there occurred the miners' general strike in 1947 and the civil servants' strike in 1953; when, at the height of the Indochina war, the PCF organized demonstrations against General Matthew Ridgway's visit to France, demonstrations that rang with shouts of "Ridgway go home!"; when several PCF leaders were arrested in the following days; when the war in Algeria provoked the fall of the Fourth Republic: then the context allowed for the dialectic described by Jean-Claude Milner.

But nothing like that exists today. As a result, the dissident intellectual, the – let's say communist, in the generic sense of the word – intellectual cannot but be in an outsider position. Lacking any real influence over the existing social and statist game, they have to work directly – and this is a new opportunity for them – to create a new politics. The road needs to be staked out, and that makes being a mere fellow-traveler impossible. But after all, that was already Marx's case, and many other people's since, in many other countries.

PP: *I'm surprised by the absence of references on both your parts to the tradition of French socialism, to the solidarist movement, to Jean Jaurès, to Léon Blum.*

JCM: *Is* there a tradition? I'm not so sure. Those references are only good for electoral campaigns. In other words, they're names that only specialists can connect with specific historical content. To judge by the use that was recently made of them, these names are only mentioned in order to inspire a vague duty in everyone to admire them. But I know enough about them to remember that they were once, on the contrary, responsible for the fiercest divisions. In Jaurès's case, assassination; in Blum's case, verbal and even physical attacks in peacetime and, during the war, deportation to Buchenwald with the status of "high-ranking" prisoner, handed over to the Germans by the French government. So, for a time, they were political names. But politics is gone from them now.

AB: In what sense was that French socialism creative and really independent of both parliamentarianism and, even more seriously, colonialism? Twice, Jaurès did in fact adopt positions that can be admired: against the French occupation of Morocco and against the mechanism of consensus that led to World War I. But his political method remained typically governed by the idea of the left as I described it. As for Blum, let's not forget that he reacted to the June 1936 strike movement as "a slap in the face" and that he refused to actively, materially, and publicly support the Spanish republican government, a legitimate government that was facing a military coup d'état and the blatant, massive intervention of the German and Italian fascist countries.

PP: *On all these issues concerning the left and the different types of socialism there don't seem to be any major differences between you. But I'd nevertheless like to explore the analysis further before we get to any disagreements you may have. Alain Badiou, in a recent lecture devoted to the contemporary, you presented in a very sequential manner each of the possible figures of commitment as they developed in the period after World War II: the Resistance and collaboration, imperialism and anti-imperialism,* gauchisme *and anti-*gauchisme, *human rights and the duty to intervene, right up until the 1990s, and you left open the possibility for new configurations as regards emancipation. You spoke of* *an "inner exile" and said you were banking on the emergence of a "disinterested interest." Given this reconfiguration of French politics, but given, too, the subjective figures that might develop, what would your prognosis be? It's unlikely that the crushing of the middle class, increasing inequality, and social fragmentation in the rich countries can be avoided, but, at the same time, new forms of resistance are emerging. I'm thinking here of Occupy Wall Street, the indignés movement, and so on.*

AB: My assessment of the global status of different forms of politics is that we are in an in-between period, which will probably last for quite a while. What I call an in-between period is one that comes after the exhaustion of a unique figure – let's call it the figure of emancipation – that has dominated people's minds as well as countries and actions over a period whose beginning can be traced back to either the Bolshevik Revolution of 1917 or the French workers' movements of the nineteenth century, or even the French Revolution, a period that was in any event dominated by the category of revolution. The word "revolution" was the basis on which huge differences of opinion over the analysis of situations, doctrinal references, the forms of organization, and so on, arose, but, as a subjective principle, it was the key term.

We need to be clear about this. I don't think anyone today knows anymore what a revolution is or can be. During what its participants called the Great Proletarian Cultural Revolution, the GPCR – and regardless of what one may think of it – the word "revolution" was still used, and that was the last time it was used in a way that wasn't vague or metaphorical.

Nobody knows what a revolution is, and the conclusion that was quickly drawn from this is that nobody knows what History is, either, anymore. Historicity itself, as subjective activity on an overall scale, has become completely unclear. We know that the figure denoted by the word "revolution" is obsolete, but we have no figure that's equivalent, even minimally, to what was thought under that name. So we're in a period of reconstruction, which is, as usual, unsettled. That's what in-between subjectivity is.

When it comes to Occupy Wall Street, what's very striking is the double weakness of the actions and, even more so, of the languages. The language is elusive. So, either you think that the right way to occupy this in-between period is for each of us, individually, to find the best place possible for ourselves in the world and just stay there, accepting the prevailing discourses, or else you think otherwise and you hold on to a bit of defiance, in which case three tasks must be completed, as I see it.

The first of these is to provide your own individual assessment that is different from the prevailing assessment of the previous period. That was the aim of my book *The Century* (2005; English translation 2007). Assuming that the planet "Revolution" is a dead planet, we need to have our own assessment of that demise and examine, on our own, the enterprises of Robespierre and Saint-Just, of Marx, Engels, Blanqui, and Varlin, of Lenin, Trotsky and Stalin, Mao and Ho Chi Minh, Castro and Guevara, of millions of people, well known or unknown, who participated in the extraordinary adventures covered by the word "revolution." Leaving all of this to be evaluated by crude reactionary propaganda is just plain crazy. We have no choice but to think this history by ourselves and fearlessly take responsibility for our own assessment of things. Any consensus about the history of revolutions is disastrous.

The second task involves formulating ideological hypotheses, intellectual propositions, with the aim of maintaining the principle of a possibility that is not reducible to the in-between figure itself. Work of this sort is both political and philosophical in nature because it's a projection into thought, into historical possibility.

The third task consists in paying extremely close attention to the whole spectrum of scattered political experiments, of local innovations, however small, that seem to be heterogeneous to the capitalo-parliamentarian order, and in paying attention on a global level, because we don't automatically know what's important or not about such experiments.

JCM: Picking up on Alain Badiou's presentation, I'd say that, of the three tasks, I could endorse two of them, namely, the patient, careful review of what took place and the attention that needs to be paid to the various new political phenomena emerging in the world.

The twentieth century took place. We should examine it in detail and discuss it, all the more so because it is becoming increasingly unintelligible. Badiou and I are basically people of the twentieth century; that's at once our strength and our limitation. It's our strength because we understand what went into making the twentieth century what it was, which is not something self-evident. I realize this whenever I give a press interview. I'm usually dealing with people who are a lot younger than I am and, in whatever I happen to be talking about, there are many points that have ceased to be clear or even able to be imagined. On top of that, there's a change of another kind: the language of which we're the vehicles is in dire straits. It was once the major language of world culture, but its status has changed to that of a minor language. We've lived through that transition. We're no longer in Sartre's position, for example. So that leads to our having to face up to the plurality of the world's languages in a way that has no precedent – or at least no precedent we can imagine. We have to innovate.

The need to go back over the twentieth century in detail reminds me of something analogous in the eighteenth century. For the French-language political thinkers, the big issue was Louis XIV. Was he a tyrant or not?

Voltaire and Montesquieu wondered about this and gave opposite answers. We need to ask ourselves whether the twentieth century was anything other than one long string of horrors. Badiou's answer and my own would no doubt differ as to the details (and yet the details are all-important here), but for both of us the question itself is legitimate.

The other task of Alain Badiou's that I would endorse is, as I said, the attention that needs to be paid to the emergence of various new political phenomena in the world. My overall perception isn't the same as his, of course, but, to give an example, we would agree, I think, about the possibility that a new kind of capitalism is developing in China and India – that is to say, in countries that are becoming major players in capitalism after having been its passive playthings under colonialism. In parallel with this, we'd tend to share, I think, a sort of lack of interest in the Wall Street *indignés* movement.

Where there's a major difference between us is on the issue of hypotheses – in other words, the second task in Badiou's list. A hypothesis, in his sense, is defined by its going beyond the "there is." I, for my part, say there's no reason, there's never been any reason, to go beyond the "there is." Since Plato's *Republic* has recently occupied Badiou's mind, let me go back to the Allegory of the Cave. As far as I'm concerned, we can never leave the cave. I identify methodologically with the prisoners who note the figures that come one after another, the series of successive resemblances, disparities, and so forth. All my thinking – and this has been the case right from the time I took up linguistics – hinges on processes of this sort. Conversely, of Alain Badiou's three tasks, the one that's based on the notion of hypothesis asserts that it's possible to leave the cave and that, since we can do so, we *must* do so. So you can gauge how wide the gap between us is. I would add that, in the system Badiou just presented, the three tasks are intimately bound up with one another. Since I don't accept one of the three, the whole thing falls apart, especially since the task that I don't accept seems to me to be the most important and characteristic one by far.

PP: *You nevertheless have a hypothesis of the end, Jean-Claude Milner: the end of the intellectual petty bourgeoisie, the end of the French language . . .*

JCM: Let's not play on words. Badiou calls any proposition that puts itself beyond the "there is" a "hypothesis." I, for my part, formulate hypotheses that pertain to the "there is." They amount to predictions, similar to those the prisoners make about the figures that may or may not appear on the screen (I'm using Badiou's explicitly cinematic interpretation of Plato's cave here).

I don't hide the fact that my analysis is based to a very great extent on a classical Marxist-type analysis. I've made some predictions about the intellectual petty bourgeoisie in France, about the fact that it exists in a special way in France as compared with other countries. Overall, these predictions haven't been disproved. In 1997 I pointed out how difficult it would be, in the case of a structural crisis, for the capitalist system to agree to pay the middle-class wages that were as high as before. I predicted that there would be a general decline in the living standard of the salaried middle class. But my hypotheses don't always entail the end of something. Thus, I predicted the emergence of a salaried middle class in India and China. That's also been confirmed.

AB: And that's moreover why, in light of the "scientific" basis of this analysis, I can validate most aspects of it. "Prediction," here, is in fact totally different from "hypothesis," in the sense I give the word.

Basically, the situation Jean-Claude Milner describes is quite simply what has gradually become obvious, namely, the tendency of the rate of profit to fall. That's what it's all about. The tendency of the rate of profit to fall, on the basis of which Marx said that capitalism had no future, has been the subject of endless debates during all the periods of capitalism's conspicuous expansion. Today we've reached the point of saturated globalization, or globalization that's in the process of becoming saturated. The areas of the world that are free from imperialist domination and the plundering of raw materials are becoming ever more scarce and are subject to fierce competition. These zones of violence and organized poverty are increasingly concentrated on the African continent, a region of enormous political chaos with no strong state, and where capitalist looters from all over the world do their shopping.

But this won't last forever. Capitalism is already unable to make a profit from the labor of all the human beings available, and so a truly gigantic reserve army of the unemployed and farmers without land is being built up on a global scale. As we well know, a significant proportion of the populations in the "democratic" countries themselves end up joining this army of the unemployed. Thus, imperialism and war, the usual remedies for the tendency of the rate of profit to fall, aren't as available as they once were, and the domestic market alternative is itself engaged in a process of decline, of which the current crisis is merely a phase. Capitalism is now forcing us to consider vast numbers of people as completely superfluous, in terms of the urgency of profit-making. Given this situation, the need for our masters to pay less to the traditional pillars of capitalism and its "democratic" political system, i.e., the upper fringe of the middle class, or even the lower fringe of the upper-middle class, is a fact of life.

But none of this amounts to a hypothesis. Indeed, it's merely an analysis of what there is, and no political orientation, nothing that can chart the way out of this "there is," can result from such an analysis alone, as opposed to what the subjective dynamic of a hypothesis can provide.

JCM: We're back to the difference between our methods here. It's a fundamental difference. As I already said, I don't think it's possible to get out of the cave. This surely comes from my past as a linguist, since linguistics, as a science, cannot escape languages as they are: it's what I call a "cave-dwelling" science, as opposed to mathematics.

AB: You could say that our positions are in some respects in the same relation to each other as the relation in which linguistics is radically distinguished from mathematics. It's a metaphor, but a metaphor that Jean-Claude Milner is right to suggest. I'd say that not only can you not get out of the cave, Jean-Claude, but on top of that, you're forced to assume the complete contingency of the cave.

JCM: I agree. When you describe the characteristic features of the anti-philosopher I think I remember that you use the word "science." You speak of anti-philosophy's lack of interest in science, which is evidenced by its lack of interest in mathematics. Whereas, as far as I'm concerned, a distinction has to be made: I hold that mathematics in itself doesn't teach anyone anything; mathematized physics and all of modern science, however, are worthy of the greatest attention. True, physics can be regarded as cave-dwelling. It wasn't so for Plato, quite obviously.

AB: And even then! Because if you consider Plato's position on mathematics as it's presented in the *Republic*, the *Theaetetus*, or the *Meno*, and if you then look at his position on cosmology in the *Timaeus*, you can see that it's not at all the same. That's because physics presupposes mathematics, even in Plato, whereas mathematics doesn't presuppose any particular physics and so is a lot closer to what could be called the neutrality of the being-multiple. In my own philosophical system

I acknowledge the cave-dwelling nature of physical science, even mathematized physical science, inasmuch as it's the science of a world, and because of the fact that it's not able to present itself as the science of any possible world, as is shown by the existence within it of purely contingent parameters (the speed of light, the mass of particles, and so on). It's the science of *this* world. But nothing in physics obliges us to consider that *this* world is *the* world.

PP: *But is it possible for that difference to be understood in another way as regards what Alain Badiou would call the exception: the possibility that chance exists in the structure of the world, which is resumed in the formula [from* Logics of Worlds*], "there are only bodies and languages, except that there are truths"? Isn't it that "except that" that the two of you disagree about?*

JCM: Is it an "except that" that makes it possible to get out of the cave? Is it an "except that" that remains inside the cave?

AB: We shouldn't lose sight of the fact that contained in "truth" is the suspensive dimension of evental chance. It is only by chance that a previously unnoticed possibility of exiting the cave opens up. However, in "truth" there is also the generic. The generic is what accounts for the fact that, from within the situation, from within the cave of appearances, there can indeed appear, under particular circumstances that I won't go into here, a type of multiple-real that can't be reduced to the particularities or the laws of the place. It is generic in this sense: it contains in itself, even though it's within the situation, a potentially universal feature. None of the available predicates of the situation make it really possible to apprehend or name or divide it. To use the metaphor that opposes us to each other, just as linguistics is opposed to mathematics, "generic" denotes that which, in the mathematical theory of multiplicities, cannot be reduced to the singularity of a language. Hence, a linguistically indiscernible multiplicity.

Now, an indiscernible multiplicity in the language of the cave, in the language of the situation, is a crucial aid for getting out of the cave, meaning: for becoming incorporated into a new truth. Why? Because what's indiscernible in the language of the situation may be of use outside, in terms of being universal. That's what I think we disagree about: Jean-Claude Milner doesn't believe that this link between the universality of the true, indiscernibility or genericity, on the one hand, and getting out of the cave, on the other, exists.

JCM: I have to stand firm on this point because I also happen to be perfectly able to allow for variations. I could say: "This is how things are, but they could be otherwise." But making this detour through the "it could be otherwise" will enable me to return to the "there is." In other words, it's true that I'm like a prisoner chained to my cave, but I'm not one of those who think that the parade of figures on the screen constitutes the only film possible: I can play with the possibilities and vary them. Consequently, there can be a consonance between what, for me, is of the nature of variation and leads back to the "there is" and what for Alain Badiou is of the nature of hypothesis and supposedly doesn't lead back to the "there is." There can be a kind of homophony.

AB: But to an even greater extent there may be a false appearance of agreement since, being a Platonist through and through, I assume that leaving the cave only serves to return to it. We must always be militants of truths, make them known, and bring those who languish in the cave around to them. So we have to go back down into the cave. In politics, this is the Maoist principle of staying close to the masses: if the intellectuals don't stay close to the workers, peasants, and low-level employees, no communist politics is possible. We'd thus have two very different systems, but both of them in a loop formation. There'd be the large loop of universality, which purports to go outside, and the small, pragmatic loop, which proposes internal variations.

PP: *If we were to take the example of debt cancellation, which is regarded by a large number of political personnel as a wise political move, if we were to take the figure of the indebted man, would this loop scheme work?*

AB: I'm not sure that example works because I think the very subject of debt cancellation as it's currently treated is still a strictly internal one. It doesn't assume the hypothesis of an exit; all it does is offer a variation, i.e., can't debt be examined under the assumption of its cancellation, its elimination, or its reduction? We know it's possible: the Greek debt was reduced by 50 percent and the world didn't come to an end. A few years ago, Argentina imposed a large-scale moratorium on its debt and surmounted the very serious crisis it was undergoing, without in the least proposing a way out of capitalo-parliamentarianism.

The figure of the indebted man has to do with a different problem, as far as I'm concerned, namely, the fate of the petty bourgeoisie. The petty bourgeoisie's support of capitalism, the fact that it's a pillar of the "democratic" system, was, and still is, based on the condition of living a life of ease on credit. Jean-Claude Milner very rightly pointed out that the capitalist system, in its current dire straits, is no longer able to provide such a life on credit in any sustained, lasting way.

JCM: Yes, there are a number of objective parameters to consider, for instance, the number of people living on earth. The talk used to be of a spiritual atom bomb, but now we've got a material atom bomb.

AB: Gaston Bouthoul [1896–1980], the old demo-
graphic theoretician of wars, would have concluded that
war is inevitable, to ensure that several tens of millions
of people are gotten rid of in one fell swoop.

JCM: I remember Peyrefitte's second book on China [*La
Chine s'est éveillée* (China Has Awakened), 1997] in
which he included an interview that he'd had with a
Chinese prime minister, the one who'd been responsible
for crushing the Tiananmen Square movement. Interest-
ingly enough, this prime minister informed him that he'd
agreed to be interviewed because Peyrefitte had encoun-
tered a similar problem in May 1968. In the course of
the discussion, the Chinese prime minister explained
what, in his opinion, was perfectly obvious, namely that
China had too large a population in relation to the
amount of arable land it possessed and that Africa was
under-populated in relation to the land *it* possessed. He
concluded that this imbalance would be resolved one
way or another. In fact, he was forecasting something
that's been happening for several years now – not necessarily through Chinese government channels but through
Chinese immigration, at any rate. In the countries of
sub-Saharan Africa all the small-scale trade is now concentrated in the hands of the Chinese. That's an example
of prediction: clearly, it doesn't get us out of the cave.

AB: In order for the debt issue to be changed into an exit
hypothesis, you'd have to imagine a political force that
would use all the means of the state – in circumstances
that I can't really imagine today – and would cancel the
debt because such would be the ineluctable consequence
of a general set of measures extremely detrimental to
private property (nationalizations, expropriations, sei-
zures, strict exchange controls, the closing of borders,
and so on). You'd obviously have to assume that this
would involve declaring a state of emergency, announcing major sacrifices, and the active and voluntary

mobilizing of the vast majority of the population. So "debt cancellation" would mean that we'd be exiting the existing system, at the cost of enormous risks for everyone – which would presuppose a state of the global system of political forces that does not currently exist.

JCM: And most likely a trade model that would be completely different from the currently prevailing system, which we aren't able to imagine.

PP: *If we combine your methods and turn to a different problem, one that clarifies your respective approaches to the issue of the state and the intellectual petty bourgeoisie – something that you, Jean-Claude Milner, call the "stabilizing class," which has in fact ceased to stabilize the state apparatus – what picture can be painted of the current state of affairs?*

JCM: Maybe I ought to remind you of my position on this. In my latest books I discuss Europe and say that one of the important phenomena concerning it is the fact that in the twentieth century it experienced the fragility of the state. In the nineteenth century it was assumed that what guaranteed a society's stability *de jure* and *de facto* was a well-conceived state. The criteria for "well-conceived" were debatable. The English conception wasn't the same as the French conception, and the French conception evolved over time: although it began with the conviction that a republican state was doomed to instability, it nevertheless ended up concluding that the most stabilizing state was a republican one. The German conception was different yet again. But it doesn't matter. Everyone agreed that the state was the quintessential stabilizer.

In the twentieth century, however, experience gave the lie to that certainty. It appeared that the state was not stable in and of itself. That was the final word of the experience of European fascisms: the state was something that could be overtaken in a matter of a few days. World War I was obviously of major importance. The countries that lost the war experienced non-stability from the perspective of defeat. The countries that won it experienced the same thing, but with a time lag. As far as France was concerned, it was 1940. Our parents' generation discovered what had previously been unthinkable for them, namely that the French state could be blown to bits. From a certain point of view, even if it wasn't experienced as a tragedy this time around, we who were children under the Fourth Republic and who lived through the transition to the Fifth Republic saw with our own eyes that the state could easily be taken over. If that was true, then it meant that the state, not being stable in and of itself, wasn't what stabilized society either.

The bourgeoisie's big discovery, prompted by the experience of the twentieth century, was that (1) it had no other choice but to be the stabilizing class itself and (2) it was possible for it to be so. I described this in terms of Europe, but it seems to me that a number of non-European countries pose the question in similar terms, i.e., if we want a stable state, don't we need a stabilizing class? Once you enter the global market, as is the case with China and India, doesn't this stabilizing class have to be structurally linked to the functioning of capitalism? Production is the first thing that comes to mind, but producers – I mean entrepreneurial-type producers – are always in a minority in a capitalist system. Consequently, they can never, on their own, stabilize the whole. Classical capitalism, as Marx described it, therefore has to be reformed, because, in the long run (this is Marx again), the largest group will be those who don't benefit from the system. *Capital* predicted that, sooner or later, those who stood to benefit from capitalism's demise would make up the overwhelming majority.

In order for the system to be stable, that logic has to be reversed. The group of those benefiting from the system has to become sufficiently numerous. Here's where what I call the "salaried middle class" comes in: it is committed to capitalism, no longer through the fragile means of land ownership or rent but through the far more direct means of wage-earning. In terms of numbers, the salaried middle class greatly exceeds the group of those who reap the benefits of surplus value directly – and, above all, it conceives of itself as having, and being able, to increase in number. That's the theme of upward mobility. But if the salaried middle class becomes a sociologically dominant class, it isn't because of a purely sociological mechanism; it's because its existence resolves the decisive issue, namely, how can a class be developed that will stabilize, through its existence and its own interests, the overall system? So there you have the notion of a "stabilizing class."

AB: The advantage of the concept of a "stabilizing class" is that it doesn't overlap with the concept of a "ruling class." I'm struck by the fact that you can't really talk about "the ruling class" today, if what is meant by that is a class that may be a very tiny minority while still being viewed as able to exert a dominance that everyone accepts. Jean-Claude Milner's suggestion seems empirically justified to me when he says that what there can be today is a "stabilizing" class rather than the traditional "ruling class." This "stabilizing class"– I'm adopting this very evocative term – is connected, to be sure, to immediate material interests, but it has neither a broad and coherent worldview, which would impress everyone, nor a prestige or refinement that would distinguish it, nor an imperialistic ideology that would give it the authority to plunge the whole country into war. "Distinction," according to Bourdieu,[6] has become an anachronism, and the participation of

[6] See Pierre Bourdieu, *Distinction*, trans. Richard Nice (Cambridge, MA: Harvard University Press, 1984).

"citizens" in a patriotic war is so unimaginable nowadays that the draft is being eliminated everywhere. There *is* a rapacious oligarchy, but it's almost anonymous. It's invisible, even though it controls the general management mechanisms of Capital. In this sense, it doesn't "rule;" it manages, it stabilizes.

The stabilizing class will run into problems – this is already happening – caught as it is between its global dependency and its national situation. I'm struck by the emergence of a large number of international employees, experts of every kind from every country, a sort of worldwide civil service of capitalist globalization. Suddenly we see someone from Harvard taking over as Mali's interim prime minister, and the same goes for Ouattara in Ivory Coast, as well as for the recent contender for power in Libya. Africa is gradually being put in the hands of direct clients of globalized capitalism, and this phenomenon shows how the internal resources of the stabilizing class are not just exceptionally weak in some places but perhaps limited all over the world, with no real prestige, and incapable of generating any enthusiasm whatsoever. So in that sense, yes, the stabilizing class is not a ruling class.

PP: *But then, when you ironically said that the stabilizing class must be stabilized, what did you mean by "must"?*

JCM: Let's say that the people with power want to go on being people with power – the opposite is rarely the case. Then let's assume that such a continuation depends on the stability of the whole whose levers they control. That's a first answer to your question: from where and from whom does the demand for stability come? But there's a second answer.

For a long period of time the source of stability was quite simply armed force. Then there was a transition from the military to the civilian, inasmuch as the source of stability was considered to be the state. What's more, that conception was called "civilized." Today, in a significant number of countries, stability is ensured by a stabilizing class. It is stabilizing not because it has military means at its disposal or because it possesses extraordinary wealth, but because its ongoing self-interest is in line with the stabilization of the way things are. The stabilizing class requires the system that puts it in the position of being a stabilizing class to be stable. This self-perpetuating machine might be called "preserving gains": that's the language the unions use, but its slogan might also be "thinking about the world of the future" or about "our children's welfare." The discourses are roughly the same, except that one is focused on the past and the other on the future.

That said, a lot of things can happen that might disrupt the processes. In particular, maintaining the stabilizing class may be too expensive relative to the surpluses generated by the current world production. The intellectual petty bourgeoisie is first in the line of fire since it only has an indirect relationship with the economy; the benefits it provides in terms of stabilization are fleeting; and the question of its cost immediately comes up. In France, the petty bourgeoisie is closely linked with the civil service. The proposals being heard today about civil servants really have to do with the intellectual petty bourgeoisie and its future (or lack thereof).

I've answered your question, but I'd like to add something else. Stability is something that's calculated. I listen religiously to the pundits on the radio every morning. "Religiously" is the word for it, since they all worship at the feet of stability. According to them, they all have definitions of the context in which the stability index should be calculated. It's an international context: global, first of all, and then subdivided into large groups, among which are Europe, the United States, China, and so on. Where these groups are concerned, stability is measured by this scale. Where Europe is concerned, they don't go down to the national level, whereas a growing number of people think the national level is the right one. It's clear that public opinion is tending in that direction in Germany. Soon we'll hear respected proponents there – on the right and/or the left – assert that it is indeed on the level of Germany that the measure of stability must be gauged. It won't take much for them to persuade a number of French politicians to adopt a similar line of reasoning. Stability is regarded as desirable by virtually everyone, but the level on which it's calculated isn't always the same, depending on the analyses. The more acute the crisis becomes, the more people will tend to define narrow zones of stability.

PP: *In that connection, what do you think about Europe's future? Integration? A federation of nation-states? A federal Europe? How is the question framed for you?*

AB: I have a point of view about this that's closely pegged to the "there is" and doesn't depend on my general hypotheses. It's a cave-like point of view, for once. The idea – often promoted by the extreme left – that a stabilization principle can be obtained from our own oligarchy by returning to a smaller scale, whether national or purely local, has, to my mind, no future, given the present circumstances. The examples that are sometimes given – Iceland or Switzerland, or even at a certain moment Japan, which was paradigmatic but then got sick immediately afterward and hasn't yet recovered – are totally unconvincing. And when you take the example of Germany, you have to remember that only a few short years ago Germany was the sick man of Europe. All of this is extremely precarious. If I were president – you can see that I'm deliberately placing myself in the worst spot in our cave – I would immediately say: "My fellow citizens, let's put an end to France, whose history is already longer than it should be. Let's merge with our German neighbor, which, as a result, will put an end to Germany, something everyone will be happy about. And then we'll scare the hell out of everyone, which is a good start for a country."

PP: *Maybe we can wind up that subject now. Alain Badiou, a conversation you had with Alain Finkielkraut ended with the following sentence: "France is finished."[7] Rather than charting a course for its revival, can each of you, on the basis of that phrase, tell us what you see ahead on the intellectual and intergenerational levels and from a broadly historical perspective?*

JCM: I think that France is above all the product of its history: in addition to its geographical location, which makes it Europe's airport, it's the culmination of a history. And the French language has a very special relationship with that history, a relationship that cannot necessarily be found anywhere else. It's true that I tend to be extremely sensitive to the fact that the twentieth century in France was a failure: all the great historical opportunities were missed. Let me stress that I'm talking only about France as a country with a history and a language, a country that has been led by a certain kind of people, with a certain kind of background, in which the rue d'Ulm [the École Normale Supérieure], of which we're products, has played a not inconsiderable – and overall disastrous – part. Regardless of whether you take the way World War I was started and the way it was treated and resolved in 1918, or World War II, or our colonial empire, it's all one big train wreck. We're faced with a wide array of failures that are not compensated for by a handful of successes. And some of the

---

[7] See Alain Badiou and Alain Finkielkraut, *Confrontation*, tr. Susan Spitzer (Polity, forthcoming).

latter were purely and simply a matter of appearances: the 10 years of De Gaulle's presidency, for example. Basically, there's only one success I regard as a genuine one – and it's being increasingly challenged, as you know: having eliminated the word "God" from the vocabulary of politics.

When people say "France is finished," what pains me, at bottom, is the issue of the language, which is something I could almost say I'm part and parcel of. When I did linguistics, I wrote my articles in English and I thought in English. So I've had the experience of thinking in a different language. And it's true that there *is* a difference. Some may argue that a difference is not necessarily a loss. Yet I think that with the French language, as it was fashioned by the twentieth century, there *is* the threat of a loss. With the disappearance of the German language in 1933, the task of thinking the twentieth century fell to the French language again, for lack of anything better. After the Third Reich, that task couldn't be undertaken in German. Italian had been Mussolini's language and, after 1945, the combined weight of the Italian Communist Party and the Catholic Church was felt heavily. Spanish – let's not even go there. It was Franco's language, the language of the Catholic Church, and that of the Latin American dictatorships all at once, and that was the case for a long time. As for English, the problem with it is not that it thinks the twentieth century in terms of the tragedies of the twentieth century, but that it thinks it in terms of the solutions the English language is a vehicle for, which is to say the market. Naturally, there are a lot of examples of the contrary, even in Anglo-Saxon philosophy, but it's true overall.

The task of thinking, of producing a careful, detailed, in-depth analysis of the events of the twentieth century, has not been completed, and I'm not sure it can go on without the French language – not necessarily *in* French, but not without that language and not without its continuing to be audible. However, with regard to French, I have the feeling that it's losing its ability to be heard, even among those who think they speak it.

AB: Among these gloomy observations about France I agree with the first point, namely, the nostalgia for our language. And it's something I experience directly on account of the fact that I'm forced to think and speak in English, only because, little by little, French, which, when I was young, was still a "language of culture" throughout the world, a language that was sufficient unto itself, has become a language that hardly anyone knows anymore and which, if it partly survives in its status as a cultural language, only does so as a dead, or quasi-dead, language. I can see no remedy for that. Owing to the vicissitudes of history, all the great languages of culture have experienced this figure of decline.

I do, however, note, and this is admittedly a precarious consolation, that there's still a worldwide interest, not in French per se, which no one speaks anymore, but in what is expressed in the French language, in its purported ability to say things, new and bold things, that aren't said anywhere else.

In this worldwide intellectual disposition, which expects something from the French, and from myself among them, there subsists a relationship with what's called "radicalism," which is in reality the world's relationship with the French Revolution, as it traversed its successive stages, such as the revolutions of 1848 and the Paris Commune but also the French Communist Party, Sartre, Foucault, May 1968, and so on.

PP: *Would you really say that's still the case?*

AB: It's still so much the case that I constantly have to throw cold water on the "radical" enthusiasm of my foreign friends and audiences by explaining to them (in English, naturally) how depressing and inconsistent with their expectations the French situation is and how nothing they think is going to happen will ever happen. But they don't want to believe me. So there is indeed still a French imaginary linked to revolutionary radicalism. And what's more, however much I may protest, I'm supposed to be a perfect illustration of the "radical" French intellectual, an excellent proof of the falsity of my own pessimism about my country.

I'm not happy about this, because it's as though my country were plagued by a sort of seductive mythology. That's why I feel duty-bound to explain that France is also a country with a long, solid conservative and reactionary tradition; that, however nice it might be to think of the Communards, we shouldn't forget that it was the Versaillais who won big-time and at an exorbitant cost; and that, even though there was May '68, it was immediately followed by the triumph of the reaction, of the counter-revolutionary and pro-American "new philosophers," and then by the reign of repressive laws against foreigners, and so on and so forth . . .

JCM: The whole world is clearly fascinated by the Queen of England. To a much lesser degree, the fascination with France is of a comparable nature – except that it's for opposite reasons. It's not the splendors of royalty but the daring exploits of the Revolution that grab people. But, yes, I can imagine the problem that that poses for you.

AB: Let's just say that, rather than feeling proud and saying, "Yes, you're absolutely right," I find myself paradoxically obliged to restrict myself to the duty of the real.

JCM: In some authors a sort of boldness or temerity of thinking is nonetheless evident. Sometimes there are things expressed in French that provoke a violent reaction in the thinking about recent history.

AB: I'd put it another way, and this is something that's particularly noticeable in the discipline I formally represent, which is known as philosophy. It's undeniable that part of the effects produced under that name in the French language are not produced anywhere else under that name, and this has been the case since the *philosophes* of the eighteenth century. Under the name "philosophy," or under peripheral names – because even "anti-philosophy," in French, is part of this domain, just as "psychoanalysis" was part of it, and "anthropology" and even "politics," in a vaguer sense – under all these names, then, things that aren't reducible to the university discourse or the media discourse are being expressed in French. This vitality that can't be reduced to academic fads and prevailing opinions is perceived by the intellectual youth of the whole world – and I can testify directly to this – as a singular phenomenon, which exerts an almost irresistible attraction on them, or at least on the fraction of them who aren't resigned to business as their inevitable fate.

PP: *But even so, doesn't that linguistic basis attest to the fact that there's a French singularity in terms of the question of the subject and subjectivation? The Anglo-Saxons approach the issue much more pragmatically. In his preface to* My France *(1991), Eugen Weber said that the distinctive feature of the French is that they are all utterly different from one another. You two are the living proof of that. But it's true that that opinion came from an English-speaking Jew from Vienna[8] who loved Alsatian wines! A French person who said the same thing would be instantly accused of congenital chauvinism. Whatever the case may be, is it possible to speak of a French singularity, if not a French exception?*

[8] Weber was from Romania.

JCM: If there *is* such a singularity, my personal position would be to say that it's historically determined. You don't have to go very far back in time to discover its source. I attach great importance to the emergence of what I'd call dialectical language. If you take a philosopher-writer like Bergson, his language bears no trace of dialectics. Then, from a certain point on, French-language philosophy would adopt a dialectical language. Later, following in its footsteps, literary criticism and even literature would do the same. The translations of Hegel, by Henri Lefebvre and later by Jean Hyppolite, can obviously be mentioned in this regard. So can Kojève's influence. It may be recalled that, in the 1950s and 1960s, Hegelo-Marxism was regarded, beyond our borders, as the requisite thinking of French-language intellectuals. It may be added that this dialectical language, which a number of people (Lacan among them) spoke and wrote, isn't spoken or written anymore today. But what matters to me is something else.

In fact, I don't care about dialectics per se. The important point is that the French language, as a language of concepts, changed in the 1930s. Dialectical language was the visible trace of this change, but its root cause was certain major events, namely, the emigration of a number of German intellectuals or ones who were influenced by the German language. I won't go into the role of the name "Jew" here; everyone knows what I think about that. I'll just say this: I have argued that the French language, faced with the task of thinking the twentieth century, had a specific part to play. But it still had to be capable of playing that part. If the French language is still capable of thinking the twentieth century today, of thinking it in relation to the revolutions of the nineteenth century and the late eighteenth century, this capacity depends on that very singular event, namely, the intrusion of dialectical language and dialectical thinking into it. This phenomenon can be given a specific date and should be seen as a consequence of Nazism.

Let me be clear. Hegelo-Marxism has died out. Dialectical language, as I said, is no longer being written. In fact, the critical period was very brief. But the change imposed on the language at that time continues to have an impact on it. It left its mark on authors who are not regarded as Hegelo-Marxists. I'd enjoy showing an English-speaking audience how "French theory" cannot be understood without this mark – which is a very honorable one since it testifies to the persistence of thought and writing in a time of darkness. I'll grant Alain Badiou that he is directly inscribed in that tradition. As for me, I understand dialectical language perfectly and can master it, if need be, even if I don't want to claim full affiliation with it. But I'm not sure it will long continue to be practiced or, above all, to be heard.

AB: That makes me want to conclude my own remarks by saying that, if the force of French philosophy was this dialecticization of the language that you're describing, then that's proof positive that the future is Franco-German. A brand-new nation, simultaneously "revolutionary," even if in a mythological way, and "dialectical," even if in a forgetful way, is a good foundation for new adventures of truth.

PP: *My final question will be a sort of uneasy tribute to the book that features a dialogue between Benny Lévy and Jean-Paul Sartre,* Hope Now *(1991; English translation 1996). What is hope now for you, Jean-Claude Milner and Alain Badiou?*

JCM: As far as I'm concerned, the categories of "hope" and "expectation" are meaningless because I have no object of thought other than the "there is." The future or the future tense are modulations on the basis of the "there is." Even though I'm by no means a Spinozist, I'd be inclined to classify hope and expectation as imaginary illusions.

AB: I don't use the word "hope" very often either, and yet I find it to be perfectly appropriate as a title for a novel [*L'Espoir*, translated as *Man's Hope*] by Malraux – a novel that has incidentally played a considerable part in my philosophical, political, and even existential tenacity. Nevertheless, whenever I'm in a position to speak to young people today who intend to cultivate a French-language intellectuality, hence to a very limited audience, I tell them, in one way or another, that it would be advantageous for them to learn the language we're talking about, that dialectical language. To learn it, first of all, because bad teachers have attempted to turn them away from it, and, second of all, because they'll then be able to freely examine whether they have any use for it regarding the world as it is. I note, with hope, that this piece of advice is being increasingly listened to.

JCM: Since we're leaving aside the issue of hope, whether felt or not, I'd say that, when combined with "hope," the word "now" means "tomorrow." I'm raising the question of the moment after. I've talked enough about the "there is," in the present, to stress the fact that the present can only be thought on the basis of the moment after. As I often say, the great book is the one that has not yet been written, and the most interesting remark is the one that has not yet been made. Given our biological limitations, this means that the most interesting remarks for me will be made by people who are yet to come. In other words, my own remarks are interesting only to the extent that they're in relation to remarks that I myself won't make.

PP: *Thank you both for your patience and for this exercise in lucidity.*

Postscript

After re-reading their discussions, Alain Badiou and Jean-Claude Milner requested that certain of their disagreements be highlighted for the reader. To that end, they exchanged the following correspondence.

1 Jean-Claude Milner's preliminary remarks

To get the discussion started, let me summarize a few differential propositions.

I'll begin with a definition. By "political name" I mean a name that requires politics to perform its founding function of preventing the killing of an adversary. So a name is all the more political to the extent that it pushes politics to its limit, namely, the question of its ability to prevent killing. A name is political not because people die on account of it (or for or against it, and so on) but because, if politics didn't exist, that name would be such that people might die on account of it. Sometimes politics gives way and killing occurs. Another way of putting this is: a name is all the more political the more deeply it divides the adversaries.

I'm quite happy to use Alain Badiou's formulation: "The twentieth century took place." But what took place for me was above all the progressive discovery that the name "worker" had stopped dividing. It had been the quintessential divider in the nineteenth century, but it ceased to be so. Why? On account of World War I. In the industrialized countries, the workers accepted mobilization and unity in the war. Lenin correctly assessed the issue, but he was mistaken in believing he could revive the divisive force of the name "worker" via the building of a workers' state. The Leninist parties were supposed to carry on the effort, each according to the specific conditions existing in the country where it operated. While the notion of a workers' movement figured prominently in the discourses, in actual fact the workers' movement continued to decline. Even worse, far from dividing, the name "worker" would actually unite: it became one of the many synonyms of social coherence.

It took Mao's political ingenuity to reconnect the name "worker" to division. In its different variations, the details of which were extremely complicated, Maoism linked the name "worker" to those violent divisions caused by the war against the Japanese or by the struggle within the Party. I won't go back over these facts, which Badiou has studied closely.

This Maoist linkage strikes me as illusory now. There still remained the unlinking and the return of the realization that the name "worker" had lost its political force. Not only did that realization return but it appears that it could have been arrived at sooner. A progressive discovery is also a retrospective discovery.

If the twentieth century took place, it's also for another reason, which is that the name "Jew" became a political name again, i.e., a divisive word. It had already been one before: I'm thinking of the Dreyfus Affair, which, in a sense, taught a whole generation about politics. But I won't dwell on that here.

Hitler reopened the question of politics' ability to prevent the killing of the adversary. He did so in connection with the name "Jew" – not in connection with that name only, but primarily in connection with it. He forced politics to give way. With the end of the war, politics was restored, but the question was not put to rest. The name "Jew" is still the major divider today, the one that summons politics to its limit.

This set of affirmative propositions leads me to formulate some criticisms.

1 I think Alain Badiou has underestimated the imaginary force of anti-Judaism, both within and outside of France.
2 Likewise, I think he has overestimated the political significance of the name "Palestinian." Let me explain what I mean. In my opinion, the name "Palestinian" only *seems* to be divisive. In fact, it creates consensus:
   • among fair-minded people (myself included), all of whom believe that the Palestinians are in distress;
   • in what the UN still refers to as "the Third World" (in this sense, the name "Palestinian" belongs to an earlier historical period but one that is still maintained in institutions);
   • increasingly within the Euro-Atlantic (i.e., the Western European and American) left.

Insofar as it is seems to be divisive, the name "Palestinian" promotes an appearance of politics. But the real question of politics appears with the name that is *really* divisive: the name "Jew."

3 I'll conclude with some questions I asked myself. Badiou is free to answer them or not.
   • Does the name "Jew" have the right to be used? My answer is: yes, it does.
   • Does it have a future or only a past? My answer is: it has a future.

- So long as nation-states exist (whether for good or ill), does this name have the right to be inscribed in the lexicon of nation-states? My answer is: yes, it may. If we think the twentieth century took place, then it must.
- Does the fact that such an inscription is necessarily inappropriate (since "Jew" is neither a state name nor a national name) constitute an insurmountable objection? My answer is: no. The phrase "Jewish state" is no more nor less a contradiction in terms than the phrases "workers' state" or "democratic state."

2   Alain Badiou's response to Jean-Claude Milner's preliminary remarks

I must confess that I've never really understood what Jean-Claude Milner – and other people – meant by "name." Still less have I been tempted by such nominalism, which has been pushed to the point where History is no more than a bare stage on which names, like ghosts, appear and disappear, independently of anyone's will.

This fetishizing of "names" seems to me to be similar, in fact, to the fetishizing of brands in business. "Nike" and "Peugeot" are names, too, after all, and, like the others, appear and disappear from the market depending on trends in capital flows and fashion.

Fashion . . . Indeed, theses like "the name 'worker' is dead" and "the return of the name 'Jew' is our event" are related to intellectual fashion. But isn't that view of the century the somewhat dried-up fruit of a small faction of the French intelligentsia between 1974 and today? Wasn't it Benny Lévy and his followers, Jean-Claude Milner among them, who, because they were disappointed that the Gauche Prolétarienne's boastful proclamations hadn't brought them to power, started to

savagely attack "the political worldview" and "progressivism," to scrap the word "worker" and many others
along with it, to turn "Jew" into a hyperbolic name,
and, in so doing, converted, with the same conviction
of being the best and brightest of their day, from the
fierce pro-Palestinians they once were to the most hard-
line Zionism, or even turned "the Arabs," without too
much nuance, into the antithesis of any new thinking?

That kind of flip-flopping has the advantage of turning
a patent failure into proof of superior lucidity and of
always being fashionably up to date. The word "worker"
was certainly out of fashion by the time the Gauche
Prolétarienne leaders realized that it was no longer a
word of the century and hadn't been – Milner now says
– since . . . 1914!

The spectral vision of history as a gallery of names is
the sophisticated form of what is so important to our
intellectuals: justifying their renegacy, as soon as that's
what's "in."

But let's look at the specific terms of the dispute.

To begin with the most factual criticisms, I want to
repeat once again that I have in no way underestimated
or denied the existence, even today, even in our country,
of anti-Semitism. I refer you to my writings and to the
actions I've taken part in concerning this issue. But what
Jean-Claude Milner, for his part, almost monstrously
underestimates, what he in fact simply denies, is the
quasi-consensual power in France, no doubt in Europe
as a whole, of the hostility toward Arabs and black
Africans, under the code word "immigrants." I challenge him to explain this discrepancy. Especially since,
to use his – bad – criteria, in the postwar situation the
number of Arab and black dead, dead because they were
young Arabs or young blacks, was out of all proportion
to the number of Jewish dead, and even more generally
to the number of "white" dead in our country as well
as in the Middle East. Might some killings be "right"?
Provided they serve the "right" name?

In fact, as regards the state of Israel's acts, the sophistical nature of the doctrine of "names" is vexing. First of all, these state-sponsored acts can no more be identified with "the Jews" than could Pétain's or Sarkozy's with "the French," even less so. Second of all, at a conservative estimate, the ratio of Palestinians killed by Israelis to Jewish Israelis killed by Palestinians is on the order of 100 to 1 in this conflict. The Palestinians are the ones who have had to flee, abandon their lands, witness the destruction of their homes, be shut up in ghettos and camps, spend hours to go from one village to another and get across walls. It's surprising that, this time, the sensitive Milner is not on the side of the speaking bodies that are being killed, humiliated, and locked up.

Given these circumstances, the issue isn't one of names that divide or unite. The issue is by what means the only just solution can be brought about: a modern state, which is to say, a state whose foundation is not identitarian but historical, a state that will settle this horrendous civil war by reuniting the two parties.

These factual comments have prepared me to say that it is simply not true that a political word is important (is a "name" – let's accept that convention) proportionate to what it divides. That would be tantamount to saying that in America today the real political name is "same-sex marriage." As for our own country, it would be more appropriate today for Jean-Claude Milner to regard "Arab" or "black," not to mention "Islam" and "Islamism," as pre-eminent names, since they clearly divide us infinitely more than does the predicate "Jew," which has become so consensual that Marine Le Pen herself – unlike her dad – wouldn't touch it with a 10-foot pole.

That's because her dad had a soft spot for the only kinds of politics we know in which the identitarian word "Jew" divides absolutely, namely, fascisms, and Nazism in particular. It could even be said that the word

"Jew" was only a pre-eminent political word, by Milner's standards, and therefore with respect to its powers of division, in Nazism and its offshoots. But does Milner perhaps think that all forms of politics are now akin to Nazism? I'll come back later to what leads his thinking to espouse a radical anti-politicism.

A name is political, I, for my part, would say, if it divides only to the extent that it inscribes the desire for a higher unity. That's why it's absolutely impossible for a political name to be the name of an identity, because an identity divides only in order to maintain, or even to purify, itself. Only an Idea divides, owing to its unifying power. No identity is universal, only what goes beyond identity toward a generic multiplicity is.

It will be objected: "But what about 'worker,' then?" "Worker" has never been an identitarian (professional, descriptive, social, etc.) name, except where it lost its political significance: in trade-unionism. The militants of the past century – but those of the nineteenth century as well – of course spoke of the "working class" or, better yet, of "the proletariat," but those words were in no way master-signifiers of *politics*. In the early twentieth century, moreover, Lenin in *What Is To Be Done?* gave the lie to this infiltration of trade-unionism (as he called it) into politics. The "workers' movement," he said, is by no means political in itself.

So what is the "real" name? It's obviously the word "communism." "Worker" is much too restrictive, its significance being only instrumental: through it pass, temporarily, a number of processes that can be guided by the communist Idea. "Proletariat" denotes the capacity of the working class for communism. And even then, that capacity isn't an exclusive one. When Mao attempted to explain the true meaning of the word "proletariat," he concluded that this was how the "friends of the revolution" – the revolution being the communist revolution – were designated. "Proletariat" is a variable predicate; the fixed point is communism.

But this is how it was *right from the start*. Marx is careful to say that he wasn't the one who invented "class struggle" or "workers' movement." His own particular contribution, in terms of the state, was the need for a transitional phase of dictatorship, and, in terms of politics, communism. His "Manifesto" was that of the Communist Party. And his International was a communist one.

This is because "communism" is a term that concerns generic humanity positively and is not an identitarian and/or a negative term, which concerns one faction, one stage, or one trend alone.

Let's say that a political word is a name if it affirms the Good, if it's an Idea of the Good, in the realm of collective action, of the historical movement reflected in an organization of that action.

In this sense, moreover, there are only two fundamental political words today (two names): "democracy," which purports to unify the world of collective life under the external law of competitive capitalism, and "communism," which purports to unify it under the immanent law of free association.

But Jean-Claude Milner, like Glucksmann,[1] *thinks only in terms of evil*. He's like Monsieur de Mun, that member of Parliament to whom Jaurès once retorted: "You like the workers, Monsieur de Mun, you like them bloody!"[2] Milner's thinking feeds on calamities. He has told us as much: the only thing one can hope for, one *must* hope for, is to put an end to massacres, to condemn killings. When it comes to "political" thought, Jean-Claude Milner has a great need for victims, bloody workers, and long-suffering peoples.

To be perfectly frank, that view of things is absolutely nothing but good old morality. Ultimately, Jean-Claude

[1] André Glucksmann is a former member of the Gauche Prolétarienne turned right-wing "new philosopher."
[2] In this play on words, "saignants" ("bloody") also means "rare," as in the degree of cooking of a piece of meat.

Milner has never experienced or engaged in the slightest politics. For a short time, he followed the fashion of Maoism, in a version that was already apolitical: don't forget that the Gauche Prolétarienne's aim, as far as the factories were concerned, was to create "apolitical grassroots action committees" [*comités de base*]. Later on, he turned his attention to victims – that was the renegades' fashion, termed "new philosophy" – and offered them his compassion. He subsumed them all under the word "Jew," which has no meaning in this case other than the gruesome piles of corpses, intended to illustrate forever, through terrifying images, the negative morality of "no more massacres."

Unfortunately, the roots of massacres lie not in the abstraction of "the killing of speaking beings" but in precise forms of politics, *which we know are only combatted effectively by other forms of politics.*

Large-scale massacres aren't like the Plague of Athens, to which Jean-Claude Milner accuses Plato of never having devoted a single line (and he was right, in my opinion, not to: to really be concerned about the Plague of Athens in Plato's time was a matter of hygiene and medicine, period). Massacres are negative figures of certain forms of politics.

But in politics the negation of negation is not an affirmation. Being opposed to massacres lacks any substance if that opposition is not sustained by the Idea of a totally different kind of politics, an Idea that alone is capable of rationally explaining the origin of massacres and alone is able to propose a form of collective existence in which perpetrating massacres is out of the question. When it comes to this issue, morality, as Sartre said, "is zilch."[3] I think that Milner's thesis, when all is

---

[3]Sartre is quoted in Simone de Beauvoir's *La Force de l'âge* (*The Prime of Life*) as saying, "La science, c'est peau de balle; la morale, c'est trou de balle" (earthy language that translates roughly as "Science is zilch; morality's an asshole."). Badiou seems to have reversed the order of the terms here.

said and done, is that politics doesn't exist, or even that it's always detrimental and the only thing that matters is the morality of the survival of bodies. That moralizing apoliticism isn't new, but it's coming back into fashion.

By contrast, here's a capsule summary of my position. What began in the nineteenth century was the word "communism." In the twentieth century it experimented with its potential superpower status, in the form of a fusion between (communist) politics and (a popular dictatorship-based) state. We need to go back to the separation between the two, which requires a sort of political (re)beginning. But my "communist hypothesis" amounts to saying that "communism" remains the key word of this (re)beginning.

Any other approach, in particular that of the moralism of the survival of bodies, comes down to endorsing, under the key word "democracy," the dominance of the unbridled capitalism whose global expansion we are experiencing, grasping the full extent of its evil as a result.

Communism or barbarism. As a "teacher by negative example," Jean-Claude Milner confirms that this is indeed the situation we're dealing with now.

3   Milner's response to Badiou's response

As soon as the name "Jew" comes up, the tone changes. My theory anticipates and explains this. Ever since Plato, one of the ways of preventing an interlocutor from speaking has been to treat them as just some specimen of a species. I'll answer as someone who isn't representative of a species and address Badiou as someone who isn't either.

Let's consider the phrase "the name 'worker'" [*ouvrier*]. This brings me back to language. "*Ouvrier*" is an adjective in "*classe ouvrière*" ["working class"]; it's a noun in "*le parti des ouvriers*" ["the workers' party"]; it's a root in "*ouvriérisme*" ["workerism"]. In all these forms, the worker is named, whereas that is not the case with "proletarian" or "proletariat."

With "the name '*ouvrier*'" I refer to all the possible designations, suppressing the grammatical differences between them. "*Juif*" is sometimes an adjective ["Jewish"] and sometimes a noun ["Jew"], sometimes written with a capital letter and sometimes not [in French]. The partial homophony makes it possible to include "*judaïsme*" ["Judaism"], "*judéité*" ["Jewishness"], and "*judaïcité*" ["Jewishness," "Jewish origin"] in all these designations. With "the name '*juif*'" I refer to all these designations, suppressing the grammatical differences between them. As a result, "*israélite*" [old-fashioned word for "Jew" or "Jewish"] is not included among them.

Under the title *The Meaning of Sarkozy*[4] Badiou showed that the name "Sarkozy" (but also "Sarkozyism," "anti-Sarkozyism," and so forth) was of no consequence with regard to what it was the name for. I agree with him about "Sarkozy," but when it comes to the name "worker," the name "Jew," and others, my approach is the exact opposite.

Furthermore, I can ask myself: are designations originally based on predication?

• As regards "the name 'Jew,'" the answer is no. Whether as an adjective or a noun, "Jew"/"Jewish" is not a predicate. I could easily show that this is connected with the fact that the original use of the name "Jew" is related to the first person.
• As regards "the name 'French,'" the answer is yes. I could easily show that this is connected with the fact that the original use of the name "French" is related to the third person.

[4]The literal translation of the French title *De Quoi Sarkozy est-il le nom?* is "Of what is Sarkozy the name?"

• As regards "the name 'worker,'" Marxism oscillated between non-predicate status (class consciousness) and predicate status (class position). By promoting the word "proletarian" Marxism at the same time promoted the predicate form (and the third person, as a result), whether it intended to or not. The task of reconverting, albeit precariously, the word "proletarian" into a first-person name fell to Mao. Or at least if I can trust the translations.

I don't hide the fact that by using the phrase "the word 'worker'" I'm taking advantage of the total homophony [in French] between the noun and the adjective. I do the same when I speak about the name "Jew," the name "French," and so on. That homophony doesn't always exist, but when it does, it's good to take advantage of it.

My general conception of names preceded the resumption of my relations with Benny Lévy: it was already operative in *Les Noms indistincts*. At that time, I hadn't yet raised the issue of the name "Jew." My interlocution with Benny Lévy was instrumental in my decision to broaden my theory of names into a theory of the name "Jew." I can't see how this itinerary affects the validity of anything I'm saying.

I'm willing to allow that, in his reflections, Alain Badiou has not underestimated the quantitative force of anti-Semitism in public opinion. But I think he *has* underestimated the fact that that force has grown and that it has grown because it has appeared in new forms, particularly in so-called informed opinion, both in France and around the world. To avoid any misunderstanding, I'm reserving the use of the term "anti-Semitism" to the old forms and the term "anti-Judaism" to the new forms. The new anti-Judaism has become a marker of freedom of thought and political freedom.

After 1945 no anti-Jewish markers could be markers of freedom; on the contrary, they were all markers of subservience. That was the Sartrian moment. But it's over now. Today, the anti-Jewish markers have become compatible with the markers of political and/or philosophical freedom. They are even tending to become a necessary condition of it. The new anti-Jews despise the old-style anti-Semites. They dream of being liberty- and liberation-lovers, and, as newcomers, they need mentors. It's only natural that they should seek them in the global university. If they can't find the requisite anti-Jewish markers in their chosen mentors, they'll make counterfeit ones, by playing on the slightest ambiguity, the slightest homonymy. By ignoring this situation, academics the world over are running a risk.

I've been criticized for saying things that are homogenizable with the demand of the masters of the market. I've replied that homogenizable doesn't mean homogeneous. I don't say that any of Badiou's remarks are either homogeneous or homogenizable with anti-Judaism. That's not where the problem lies. It lies in the transformation of the discourse that we are witnessing today.

More broadly speaking, I realize that I need to clarify what I'm claiming about the divisiveness or nondivisiveness of a name. It's not just a question of the divisions that can be observed in public opinion. The kind of division I have in mind is basically a subjective one. Its effect is to divide subjects among themselves, but also to divide an individual subject against him or herself. The name "Jew" possesses this feature: not only does it divide public opinion but it also divides subjects against themselves – and especially those subjects who might say of themselves that they're Jewish.

By contrast, if you consider the names that ordinary divisions are organized around, they function in exactly the opposite way: they unite every subject around a central core. They divide, of course, but only so as to unite – to unite groups, but also to unite individuals around themselves. To borrow Lacan's language, I'd say that these divisions have to do with the ego ideal, not with the subject. They may sometimes empirically express divisions between subjects, but more often than not that isn't the case. Thus, the division induced by the issue of same-sex marriage confirms the image that the person who has made a choice has of him or herself. The same is true for most of the examples Alain Badiou brings to bear against me. But the division induced by the name "Jew" is of a wholly different nature.

In this regard, the word "worker" no longer gives rise to a subjective division. It's not a political word anymore. Marx's assessment of the peasants in France in the nineteenth century was similar. Linking such assertions to a doctrine of Evil seems irrelevant to me.

If I don't mention immigrants it's for a very simple reason: the main player involved is government power. On an almost daily basis any private individual can read the *Journal officiel* [the official gazette of the French Republic, which publishes statutes and decrees, parliamentary debates, etc.], or police blotters, or professional politicians' statements. They can express themself publicly on the basis of these facts, either in the press or by writing a book. Badiou does so, but I don't, because I've decided not to. Since I don't, I think it's completely pointless for me to say anything.

Now let's consider the issue of the existence or nonexistence of a nation-state that presents itself as a Jewish state. To the extent that the word "Jew" is involved, the issue sometimes gives rise to a subjective division. Sometimes it divides subjects against themselves. I've observed this in some of those who accept the principle of such a state's existence. I've been told that the same division can be observed in some of those who reject it.

I don't want to dwell on the possible overlap between the rejection of such a state and anti-Judaism. That overlap does exist, but I won't insult Badiou by ascribing it to him. Who can deny that the birth of that state was immediately followed by a war? That war is still going on. Who can doubt that it's causing many deaths?

It couldn't be otherwise. The Palestinians who are dying are convinced that they're dying on account of Israel's existence. There's no doubt they're convinced of this. But nothing proves that they're right.

Today, the Palestinians are being killed so that the current regimes in neighboring states can remain in power. This is why I think that the division induced by the Palestinians comes down to a consensus, of which the automatic majority in the UN is one indication among others. Furthermore, the changes we're witnessing today in the Near and Middle East are of course accompanied by threats against Israel's existence, but they're also accompanied by the consigning of the "Palestinian cause" to oblivion. The new regime in Egypt announced – whether it's true or not – that it would take charge of Israel's destruction by itself; as a result, the word "Palestinian" has been wiped out. This proves that the Palestinians are not dying for themselves. They're dying so that their putative allies and their putative leaders can continue to be indifferent to their fate.

Since I've been requested to provide a certificate of sensitivity, I'll admit that this state of affairs upsets me, because it is thoroughly shot through with lies, the lies that make Palestinians murmur, as they die, that it's Israel that killed them. No, it's these very lies that kill the Palestinians.

In parallel with this, Israelis often think they're dying on account of the Palestinians. That's clearly wrong. They're dying because they're identified as Jews and because certain powerful interests need Jews never to be sure whether their survival is guaranteed or not. Faced with this, Badiou talks about a modern state whose foundation would not be identitarian but historical. In my view, that proposition is just as much a rational fiction as the communist hypothesis. It could only make sense if Badiou were granted his whole system, which I don't grant him. Who can imagine that such an island of exceptionalism could survive in a region made up of states with an identitarian foundation, where the historical and the identitarian constantly overlap? Who can imagine that anything might be settled between Israelis and Palestinians when Syria, Egypt, Iran, Iraq, and so on are riddled with instability? Nowhere in the world is it possible to do any better than just cobble things together; in this area of the world such bricolage cannot go any further than achieving an armistice. The terms of the armistice cannot include the abolition of this state that calls itself a "Jewish state" and has invented its own language. The surest way to ruin an armistice and cut it short is to aim at an ideal of permanent peace.

Does that constitute allegiance to a doctrine of Evil? I admit that I regard the course of world events as being doomed to perpetual disorder, but equating disorder with Evil is Platonism. And I'm not a Platonist.

4 Badiou's three final points

First, I don't think the tone of the discussion changed because the word "Jew" came up. It changed because, with the assessment of a sort of essence of the twentieth century, of what took place in its having-taken-place, we arrived at the very heart of an absolute subjective disagreement between us. I wrote a whole book on the century, and Milner did a very good job of explaining why discussing the century is the proper task of the French language. Between my proposition, which opens up the nineteenth century to a third stage of the communist hypothesis, and his, which sees in it nothing but the meaningless emergence of miscellaneous names against a backdrop of perpetual disorder, there was no way our incompatibility could remain in the innocuous style of an exchange of opinions.

Second, nor do I think that, just because the purpose of a name is to create a non-existent unity or recreate a shattered unity and that it's divisive for this very reason, its effects can be reduced to those of the imaginary ego rather than the subject. It's obviously just the opposite. Every day I see at first hand how the key word "democracy," in its capitalo-parliamentary guise, unifies only by being based on extraordinary subjective and objective violence, which can go as far as torture and war in subservient countries but is always on the verge of insult and segregation even here. And who can't see that that word divides even me, as a subject, given that I have to assert that what's involved in the becoming of the word "communism" is a higher variant of the implicit word "democracy," of its actual realization? The political field today is on a global scale for any Subject constituted within it: (capitalo-parliamentarian) democracy versus (politico-communistic) democracy. Marx, Lenin, and Mao all got caught up in this perilous division, which is immanent to the subjective process of real communism.

Finally, in terms of the national issue, I don't think it makes any sense, in our day and age, to cling to the identity of peoples and languages, if not of races, religions, traditions, and various forms of subservience. The future belongs to generic human groups, to the acceptance of many different identities everywhere, given that, as compared with the universal, generic norm conveyed – often against states – by a genuine politics, these identities are irrelevant. In the contemporary world, the continual carving up of weak states on identitarian pretexts (Slovaks against Czechs! Flemish against Walloons! Montenegrins against Serbs! Ivoirians against Burkinabés! And so on ad infinitum) is nothing but senseless savagery, completely in the service of the combined appetites of big corporations and powerful, continent-wide countries. The lesson the universality possessed by the word "Jew" will teach this world being ravaged by capitalism is that it must inscribe in its becoming the fact that to be a Jew cannot mean to put up walls, to live only among yourselves, to cave in to the traditionalists' imprecations, to herd foreigners into camps and shoot on sight the pitiful co-inhabitants of your land who attempt to climb over your barbed-wire fences.

Bibliography

Badiou, Alain. *Being and Event*. Translated by Oliver Feltham. London and New York: Continuum, 2006.

Badiou, Alain. *Polemics*. Translated by Steven Corcoran. London and New York: Verso, 2006.

Badiou, Alain. *The Century*. Translated by Alberto Toscano. Cambridge, UK and Malden, MA: Polity, 2007.

Badiou, Alain. *Le Concept de modèle*. New edition. Paris: Fayard, 2007.

Badiou, Alain. *Le Fini et l'infini*. Paris: Bayard, 2010.

Badiou, Alain. *Entretiens 1: 1981–1996*. Paris: Nous, 2011.

Badiou, Alain. *The Rebirth of History: Times of Riots and Uprisings*. Translated by Gregory Elliott. London and New York: Verso, 2012.

Badiou, Alain. *Circonstances 7. Sarkozy: pire que prévu*. Paris: Éditions Lignes, 2012.

Badiou, Alain. *Philosophy for Militants*. Translated by Bruno Bosteels. London and New York: Verso, 2012.

Badiou, Alain. *Plato's Republic*. Translated by Susan Spitzer. New York: Columbia University Press, 2013.

Badiou, Alain, Éric Hazan, and Ivan Segré. *Reflections on Anti-Semitism*. Translated by David Fernbach. London and New York: Verso, 2013.

Badiou, Alain and Alain Finkielkraut. *Confrontation*. Translated by Susan Spitzer. Cambridge, UK and Malden, MA: Polity, forthcoming.

Banfield, Ann and Daniel Heller-Roazen. "Interview with Jean-Claude Milner." Translated by Chris Gemerchak. *Journal of the Jan Van Eyck Circle for Lacanian Ideology Critique* 3 (2010): 4–21.

Beauvoir, Simone de. *La Force de l'âge*. Paris: Gallimard, 1960.

Bernanos, Georges. *A Diary of My Times*. Translated by Pamela Morris. London: Boriswood, 1938.

Bizot, François. *The Gate*. Translated by Euan Cameron. New York: Vintage, 2004.

Bizot, François. *Facing the Torturer*. Translated by Charlotte Mandell and Antoine Audouard. New York: Alfred A. Knopf, 2012.

Bourdieu, Pierre. *Distinction*. Translated by Richard Nice. Cambridge, MA: Harvard University Press, 1984.

Crépu, Michel. *Le Souvenir du monde: Essai sur Chateaubriand*. Paris: Grasset, 2011.

Dardot, Pierre and Christian Laval. *Marx, prénom Karl*. Paris: Gallimard, 2012.

Derrida, Jacques. *Adieu to Emmanuel Lévinas*. Translated by Pascale-Anne Brault and Michael Naas. Stanford, CA: Stanford University Press, 1999.

Descartes, René. *The Passions of the Soul*. Translated by Stephen H. Voss. Indianapolis, IN: Hackett Publishing Company, Inc., 1989.

Foucault, Michel. *The Order of Things*. Translated by Alan Sheridan. New York: Vintage, 1973.

Freud, Sigmund. *Totem and Taboo*. Translated by James Strachey. New York: W.W. Norton & Co., 1962.

Guizot, François. *De la Peine de mort en matière politique*. Paris: Fayard, 1986.

Koyré, Alexandre. *From the Closed World to the Infinite Universe*. Baltimore, MD: Johns Hopkins University Press, 1957.

Lardreau, Guy and Christian Jambet. *L'Ange*. Paris: Grasset, 1976.

Lenin, V. I. *What Is To Be Done?* New York: International Publishers, 1969.

Lévy, Benny. *Le Nom de l'homme*. Paris: Éditions Verdier, 1984.

Leys, Simon. *The Chairman's New Clothes*. Translated by Carol Appleyard and Patrick Goode. New York: St. Martin's Press, 1977.

Malraux, André. *Man's Hope*. Translated by Stuart Gilbert and Alastair MacDonald. New York: Grove, 1979.

Marx, Karl. *Capital*. Volume I. Translated by Ben Fowkes. New York: Penguin Classics, 1992.

Marx, Karl. *Grundrisse: Foundations of the Critique of Political Economy*. Translated by Martin Nicolaus. London and New York: Penguin, 1993.

Marx, Karl and Friedrich Engels. *The Communist Manifesto*. New York: W.W. Norton & Company, 1988.

Milner, Jean-Claude. *Constat*. Paris: Éditions Verdier, 1992.

Milner, Jean-Claude. *La Politique des choses*. Paris: Éditions Navarin, 2005.

Milner, Jean-Claude. *Les Noms indistincts*. Paris: Éditions Verdier, 2007.

Milner, Jean-Claude. *L'Arrogance du présent*. Paris: Grasset & Fasquelle, 2009.

Milner, Jean-Claude. *Clartés de tout*. Paris: Éditions Verdier, 2011.

Milner, Jean-Claude and François Regnault. *Dire le vers*. Paris: Seuil, 1987.

Peyrefitte, Alain. *La Chine s'est éveillée*. Paris: Fayard, 1997.

Regnault, François. *Conférences d'esthétique lacanienne*. Paris: Agalma, 1997.

Sartre, Jean-Paul. *Colonialism and Neocolonialism.* Translated by Steve Brewer, Azzedine Haddour, and Terry McWilliams. New York: Routledge, 2006.

Sartre, Jean-Paul. *Critique of Dialectical Reason,* Vol. 1. Revised edition. Edited by Jonathan Rée. Translated by Alan Sheridan-Smith. London and New York: Verso, 2004.

Sartre, Jean-Paul. *Nausea.* Translated by Lloyd Alexander. New York: New Directions, 2007.

Sartre, Jean-Paul. *Anti-Semite and Jew.* Translated by George J. Becker. New York: Schocken, 1948.

Sartre, Jean-Paul and Benny Lévy. *Hope Now.* Translated by A. van den Hoven. Chicago: University of Chicago Press, 1996.

Weber, Eugen. *My France.* Cambridge, MA: Belknap Press, 1991.

Weber, Max. *Science As a Vocation* and *Politics As a Vocation.* Translated by Rodney Livingstone. In *The Vocation Lectures.* Edited by David S. Owen and Tracy B. Strong. Indianapolis, IN: Hackett Publishing Company, 2004.